PLAY
THERAPY
Activities

PLAY THERAPY Activities

101 Play-Based Exercises to Improve Behavior and Strengthen the Parent-Child Connection

By **Melissa LaVigne, LCSW, RPT**

Illustrations by **Irene Freitas**

ROCKRIDGE PRESS

Interior and Cover Designer: Suzanne LaGasa
Art Producer: Sue Bischofberger
Editor: Sam Eichner
Production Editor: Ruth Sakata Corley

Illustrations © Irena Freitas, with the exception of the following: Robin Boyer (dinosaur and fish), p. 33; Pixejoo/Creative Market (flower), p. 33; PassionPNGcreation/Creative Market, p. 51; Sarah Rebar, pp. 69 and 75; Travis Stewart, p. 113; and ViSnezh/shutterstock, p. 167.

Author photo courtesy of Karen Monaco

ISBN: Print 978-1-64739-126-3 | eBook 978-1-64739-127-0

R1

I dedicate this book to my favorite M's, for keeping life sweet, challenging, and exciting.

CONTENTS

INTRODUCTION

It was one of those moments you never think will happen until, in a split second, it does.

I had turned around for just a moment, and in that time my 18-month-old daughter had climbed at warp speed up the stairs to the first landing of our stairwell. Moments later, I heard a crash and turned to see her rolling down the stairs. In a panic, I rushed over to her, screaming for my husband to call 911. He scooped us both off the floor, offering us support as my daughter cried out of sheer terror and pain, and I cried out of fear and shame. He calmly soothed her, carrying her to the kitchen to get her boo-boo bunny, a stuffed animal filled with an icepack, to place on her now swelling lip. I took a few deep breaths and joined them in the kitchen. Reflecting back her emotions, I said: "I wonder if that was scary for you" and "You were so brave to try to climb up the stairs, but you fell and it was scary." She settled down quickly and snuggled into my arms as we called the doctor. She showed no signs of injury other than her bumped lip. We were simply instructed to keep an eye on her.

A few weeks later, I came home from work to find my husband standing at the bottom of our stairway picking up multiple stuffed animals. My daughter was standing at the top of the stairs on the other side of the closed gate.

He looked up and said, "We've been doing this all day. She just keeps throwing them down the stairs!"

Naturally, he was a bit annoyed; he didn't really want to play fetch with her. I paused for a moment as I watched her throw the toys down the stairs again. Then it dawned on me. She needed to *play* about what happened—the scary moment of falling down the stairs. As she threw them down the stairs, I vocalized how they might be feeling.

"Oh no, Elmo is falling down the stairs. I wonder if he is feeling scared."

After Elmo tumbled down, I walked calmly down the stairs to get the toys. "I want to check on Elmo and make sure he is okay, not hurt or scared," I said.

I picked up the stuffed animal and asked him if he was okay, carried him into the kitchen, and checked all over his body. My daughter followed behind me, watching intently. I asked her to help me check on Elmo. I also asked if she thought he needed the boo-boo bunny; she agreed he did.

We took turns holding the bunny-shaped ice pack on Elmo and making sure he was okay. We played this game on and off for about two weeks, always concluding it by checking in on and caring for the stuffed animal. The last time we played, my daughter initiated the game. During a diaper change, she said, "Elmo boo-boo!" At first, I wasn't sure what she was saying or what she meant. But after a moment I realized she wanted to give Elmo her bunny-shaped ice pack. She sat in my lap, and we took turns caring for Elmo's imaginary boo-boos. She paid close attention to Elmo's mouth, often placing the ice pack in the same place she'd experienced her own pain. After caring for Elmo, I said, "The mommy wants to keep Elmo safe, so she won't let him fall down the stairs like that again." That was the last time we played the game, and since then she has shown no fear or distress related to stairs or climbing.

This experience confirmed something I have always believed as a clinician but hadn't yet validated in my own personal parenting experience: Play is the true language of children. If we can learn to listen and speak the language of play, we can help our children overcome some of life's greatest challenges.

Play is one of the first ways we interact with the world, solve problems, and create connections. This is true in both humans and animals. The director of the National Institute of Play, Stuart Brown, MD, determined that play not only serves as a cornerstone for child development, but has the ability to ignite an individual's greatest potential throughout their life. As Richard Gaskill and Bruce Perry reported in their 2013 paper, "The Neurobiological Power of Play," research shows that a person's ability to play into adulthood impacts overall joy, physical health, and life satisfaction. No matter the age, the human brain benefits and thrives from engaging in play.

As a licensed clinical social worker and registered play therapist, my professional experience ranges from school settings, to community mental health, to intensive trauma treatment, to my private practice. Though I see patients of all ages, helping to meet the needs of children has always been a cornerstone of my career. And no matter the setting or client population, my play therapy skills and techniques, in particular, have come to the fore. To this day, play-based interventions continue to be some of the most effective tools in my practice.

The goal of this book is simple: to open the play therapy toolbox for parents and caregivers, so you can feel more equipped to engage playfully with your child. Integrating art, music, movement, mindfulness, storytelling, and other techniques grounded in play therapy, the 101 activities included here can increase your child's self-awareness, emotional regulation, impulse control, creativity, imagination, and ability to connect with themselves and others in a developmentally appropriate fashion. At the most fundamental level, it is my hope that these joyful interactions will strengthen the bond between you and your child.

HOW TO USE THIS BOOK:
PLAY VS. PLAY THERAPY

Before you use this book with your child, it's important to clarify the crucial distinction between play and play therapy. Although play in any form is powerful, healing, and facilitative of a child's cognitive development, the difference between normal play and play therapy is the objective: when a therapist engages a child in play-based therapy, it is specifically to help a child heal from a traumatic experience, overcome generalized anxiety, increase their ability to manage their emotions, improve family dynamics, boost their self-esteem, and/or address other specific psychological needs. Of course, spontaneous play, of the kind that parents naturally engage in with their child, can meet these needs as well. But play therapists *intentionally* work with children to achieve these goals.

Consequently, it's imperative to note that this book is *not* a substitute for actual play therapy and should not be considered a form of treatment for disorders such as attention deficit/hyperactivity disorder (ADHD) or post-traumatic stress disorder (PTSD). That said, any well-intentioned parent or caregiver should be encouraged to engage their child in the kind of intentional play activities featured in this book. Our current society continues to push children away from play, whether it's due to the prevalence of screens or a school's decision to limit recess. This book can help you re-introduce your child to the play their brains and bodies crave!

This book features 101 easy-to-follow activities, thoughtfully curated to ensure there is something for every child. However, not every activity will be right for every child. Some activities are more suitable for younger children, ages three to five, whereas others are more appropriate for older children, ages six to nine. Some activities help your child slow down, while others work to energize your child. As the expert on your child, you are encouraged to pick and choose the activities that will best meet their needs, both in the moment and based on their development.

IF YOU'RE A PARENT OR CAREGIVER

As I noted in the Introduction, this book is tailored for parents and caregivers to use with their children. If you're totally new to the concept of play therapy, the first two chapters will provide you with an understanding of the therapeutic framework that supports play-based techniques, and why your child stands to benefit from the activities featured in chapters 3 through 9. I will also help you decide whether you should seek out an actual play therapist for your child. Even if your child does not need additional play therapy support, the activities throughout this book can enrich any child.

If your child is already engaged in play therapy, this book can offer great support throughout the duration of their treatment. Due to the hectic nature of our daily lives, many of the parents I work with in my own practice struggle to remember (and apply) what we've discussed week-to-week. Use this book as a way to bring the themes and goals of treatment home, and practice play-based engagement with your child between sessions!

IF YOU'RE A PLAY THERAPIST

Although the activities in this book have been adapted to allow parents and children to engage in playful connection without the support of a therapist, they could be easily incorporated into a traditional play therapy session. Whether you provide play therapy in a school, private practice, or community mental health setting, these activities have enough variety to meet the needs of your clients.

Another powerful way to integrate these activities into active treatment is by having parents practice them with their children in between sessions; the digestible descriptions and step-by-step instructions give parents the information they need to successfully implement these beneficial techniques at home.

CHAPTER ONE

A Caregiver's Guide to Play Therapy

Before integrating the activities in the later chapters into your child's life, it's important to first understand what play therapy is, what benefits play-based activities can have for your child, and precisely why they can be so effective. This crucial context will not only help you make the most of this book, but will help you decide whether you wish to seek the help of a professional play therapist.

What Is Play Therapy?

In a world where kids are constantly being asked to listen, sit still, and meet the expectations set by adults, it can be easy to forget that they're not just grown-ups in smaller bodies. Children interact with the world differently because they *are* different. They even speak a different language than we do—the language of play.

Children use play as a way to manage emotions, develop insight, solve problems, spark joy, and, most importantly, communicate. They use play to share their biggest fears, convey their worries, and interpret the world around them.

A recognition of and respect for this truth is what led to the institution, in the 1940s, of one of the most powerful therapeutic tools for children: play therapy. Using the definition laid out by the Association for Play Therapy (APT), we can consider play therapy as "the systematic use of a theoretical model to establish an interpersonal process wherein trained play therapists use the therapeutic powers of play to help clients prevent or resolve psychosocial difficulties and achieve optimal growth and development." Mental health professionals trained in this skill use it as a tool to help children overcome many of their challenges, such as emotional regulation, anxiety, big life changes, trauma, and grief. Play therapy has the power to help a child communicate their feelings about a situation and work through them; it can also give children developmentally appropriate tools to understand and interpret their internal world. This is a vital skill in the development of social skills, decision making, and the management of emotions.

To decide how best to meet the needs of a client, therapists tend to align themselves with a particular theoretical framework. Play therapy has two primary theoretical frameworks (though many more exist): non-directive and directive. As not all play is the same, these theoretical models allow the therapist to determine which kind best addresses a child's needs.

Non-Directive Play Therapy

According to the 2010 book, *Child-Centered Play Therapy*, the idea of non-directive play therapy, developed by Virginia Axline in the 1940s, is based on the theory that children will use their natural medium of play to best express a problem they have to the therapist. In non-directive play therapy, therapists allow the child to take the lead and don't interfere with the play.

At the start of each session, the therapist will indicate that, in the playroom (see page 5), the child can play with the toys in any way they like; this statement shifts the power to the child and places the child and therapist on an even footing. As in talk therapy, where a therapist would allow the client to share information on their own terms, the play therapist trusts the child will use the language of play to communicate their worries, fears, and concerns, emphasizing the equality and safety of the therapeutic relationship.

In a non-directive therapeutic relationship, the therapist verbally tracks what the child is doing, not unlike a play-by-play announcer during a sports telecast. Through tracking, the therapist will offer support, amplify themes related to the child's symptoms, and create opportunities to overcome challenges.

In one non-directive session I conducted, a young boy was able to express and overcome his anxiety related to school. He started by building a small classroom scene in the sandtray. He placed animal figures at each desk, paying special attention to a small dog. He proceeded to share that the little dog was having some big feelings. Tracking, I said, "The little dog has some big feelings." He shared that the dog was nervous about being at school so far away from his dog mom. I wondered aloud how the little dog could get stronger, so that he could handle being at school. The client put a superhero figure in the sandtray, next to the little dog. He said that the superhero would help train the little dog and make him stronger. The client proceeded to engage the dog and superhero figure in a special training session, playing the scenario out in a few subsequent sessions. Within a month, his parents and teachers both saw a notable decrease in his school-related anxiety.

Directive Play Therapy

Directive play therapy is a method in which the therapist directs the client through a specific activity. In this method, the therapist often takes a more general therapeutic tool, such as calming strategies or problem-solving, and uses it in a play-based way. Therapists can use these activities to help clients build a specific skill, target a specific moment in time, get a child ready to work on processing a traumatic event, assess a particular issue, identify feelings, learn emotional regulation tools, or build understanding on a topic; they can incorporate art, movement, music, games, toys, role-play, snacks, and, at times, parents or caregivers. Many play therapists mix directive activities into non-directive sessions, engaging the client in the activity while verbally tracking throughout.

One of my favorite directive activities involves teaching children how to connect to their bodies; as pediatric psychologist Mona Delahooke points out in *Beyond Behaviors*, creating internal connection is a vital tool in developing emotional regulation skills. In this activity, children learn about the tiny investigator that lives inside each of us. This investigator helps them answer the question, "How does this make me feel?"

When I first introduce this concept, clients draw a picture of what they imagine their investigator looks like. Later, we experiment with different movements to see if our investigator can notice our body sensations. We engage in big, silly movements, such as spinning around in the chair, doing jumping jacks, or having a dance party. Throughout the activity, we stop and do a body check, asking our body investigator questions like, "How do my legs feel after running all around the room?!" This is a playful way of teaching a powerful skill.

It is imperative to reiterate that, although this book includes many directive activities, it is not a form of play therapy. If these activities are to be used for a therapeutic purpose, they would have to be integrated into a play therapy session by a trained professional.

WELCOME TO THE PLAYROOM

Regardless of the approach the therapist takes, the child needs access to tools (i.e., toys) they can use to speak through their language of play. This is where the playroom comes in.

A typical play therapy space is lined with open shelves, filled with miniatures that depict all aspects of life. You might find small, kind animals, like bunnies and puppies, and large, fierce animals, such as tigers and dragons. Nestled on these shelves would also be human figurines, depicting the various roles people play in society, both real and imagined: community helpers, parents, kids, grandparents, superheroes, villains, princesses, fairies, and others.

In addition, most play therapists have miniature versions of medical items, dollhouse furniture, trees, fences, bridges, rocks, and more. This wide variety of miniatures would often be used to build scenes and tells stories in the sandtray, which allows for expression in a miniaturized way. Per *Directive Play Therapy Theories and Techniques*, miniaturized play helps kids feel bigger and stronger in relation to overwhelming problems. When kids are able to take a big problem and make it feel smaller by projecting it onto a tiny toy and placing it inside a container, such as a sandtray, they feel more capable of solving said problem.

Play therapists may also have toys children can use for role-play or the dramatization of a situation. These would include puppets, baby dolls, play food, a doctor set, and dress-up materials. Craft materials, sensory toys, and other classic toy items, such as musical instruments and board games, are also quite common.

Remember that a play therapy playroom is different than your playroom at home: The goal of the play therapist's office is to allow the child to communicate without having to use words. Although it's great to offer many of these toys for your child at home, it's often not realistic!

How Does Play Therapy Work?

The therapeutic process performed through the use of play therapy is extremely powerful. I have witnessed many children overcome some of life's greatest challenges through continued parent support and engagement.

Every therapist is different in the way they structure their process, but most agree that everything is based on the individual child. Some therapists prefer to schedule an individual session with the parent(s) first, to get a sense of their concerns and the child's family history. As it is always best not to speak about the child in front of the child, planning a parent session gives parent(s) an opportunity to speak freely about their child.

During the first session with the child, the therapist will typically start by sharing basic information about confidentiality, session structure, and the role of counseling. Sessions typically last for an hour, and most play therapists will meet with new clients on a weekly basis. I like to explain to children that I am a play therapist, which is kind of like a teacher, but instead of teaching kids about math or reading, I teach kids about what to do if they are mad, sad, or worried. During this first session, therapists introduce children to the playroom and often engage in an assessment-based play, which allows them to better understand the child. Most sessions will have a similar structure, depending on the child's needs.

I typically spend a large portion of the sessions with just the child, engaging them in both non-directive and directive play activities, though I often engage the parent and child in games together to help strengthen their relationship or build skills. Parental involvement is completely based on the child's needs and goals of treatment; some parents will be present the majority of the session, whereas others will not. It is critical for the therapist to continuously check in with the parent, to offer support regarding the problem they are trying to address, as well as to track progress through the parent's reports.

Who Can Become a Play Therapist?

Any mental health professional can become a registered play therapist (RPT), including social workers, psychologists, mental health counselors, art therapists, professional counselors, school counselors, and so on.

The process can appear lengthy, but it's during this process that professionals learn vital treatment skills. To become registered, an individual must complete 150 hours of training and coursework in play therapy, in addition to 35 hours of consultation with a therapist who is a credentialed, registered play therapist supervisor. This supervisor must attest to the professional's completion of supervision hours, as well as 350 play therapy–specific clinical hours.

WHAT IS THE PARENT OR CAREGIVER'S ROLE IN PLAY THERAPY?

The parent or caregiver's role in the play therapy process is vital in children reaching their treatment goals. Although play therapists have specialized skills and training, they will never have the expertise on your child that you have. As a result, the therapist will rely on you to gather as much information as possible about your child at the start of treatment, including their prenatal and birth experience; how they interact with others (peers, adults, and siblings); how they react to different situations, such as mealtime, homework, and losing a game; and much more.

More specifically, parents play a large role in building the treatment plan—essentially, the goals of treatment. This often starts with the question, "How would you know your child is done with treatment?" Most parents are able to identify the problems and see what changes they are hoping to achieve by filtering treatment goals through that lens. Common goals include increased emotional regulation, meaning a child's ability to manage their emotional state and emotional reactions; increased knowledge and use of self-calming strategies; boosted self-esteem; or better impulse control. That said, any treatment goals will be based specifically on your child's presenting problem. For example, if your child is experiencing nightmares related to PTSD, a treatment goal might be to improve sleep by working through past traumatic events.

It is important to note that even though parents play a vital role in play therapy, the therapist will conduct many sessions alone with the child. Many children often feel the need to act like they are doing better than they are to their parents; by being alone with the therapist, the child can work through their issues without feeling the pressure to please parents.

Some aspects of treatment are impossible, however, without direct parent involvement. In this case, many therapists will split sessions between individual time and family time. A strong bond between the child and therapist will only increase the therapist's ability to offer healing tools to a child. Of course, this relationship is in no way intended to compete with or threaten the one a child has with their parent.

Can Your Child Benefit from Play Therapy?

In some capacity, everyone can benefit from the power of play!

While play-based treatment is most often used with children, it can even offer therapeutic healing for adults struggling with anxiety, trauma-related symptoms, or mood disorders. (To reiterate, though, the purpose of this book is to offer tools for children between the ages of three and nine.)

Ultimately, any child in need of mental health support would benefit from this type of treatment. Common mental health issues for which play-based inventions are used include anxiety, depression, ADHD, PTSD, any trauma-related symptom, attachment-related disorders, and/or disassociation.

If you believe your child might be struggling with one of these problems, it is a good idea to seek out treatment (see "Choosing a Play Therapist," page 11). It is always best to check with your child's pediatrician first.

Why Is Play Therapy So Effective?

Simply put: play therapy is effective because it meets children at their developmental stage, creating an avenue for healing that is based on what their brain needs in the moment.

Play is one of the many vital components of a child's healthy brain and nervous system development. It impacts the development of a child's ability to regulate their emotions, create connections, and build executive function skills. It is the natural way children explore their world, problem-solve, and develop social skills, as well as overcome challenges, engage with others, and express their needs. As it's rooted in our most primitive self, play also nourishes our brains and nervous systems long after childhood.

Play therapy may help where other forms of therapy may not. When children are under duress, their brains may jump into "protection mode." In this state, observes Mona Delahooke in *Beyond Behaviors*, they can't access the thinking part of their brain—the part of the brain that engages in the kinds of executive functions and task management required to handle the demands of everyday life, like following directions and sitting still. Cognitive behavioral therapy, for example, often only engages the "thinking brain." But if a child cannot turn their thinking brain on, no amount of "thinking" things out will help them change their behaviors. During play, children effectively bypass their thinking brain, which allows them to access their jumble of feelings and work to overcome challenges.

Play therapy is an approach rooted in joyful playful engagement. During play therapy, children laugh and often act silly. This is good therapy, and not just because of the age-old phrase, "Laughter is the best medicine." When a child is able to be themselves without the pressure of performance, and laugh along the way, they are more capable of connecting with others. And when a child connects with others in a safe way, they are more capable of accessing the parts of their brains that need healing.

CHOOSING A PLAY THERAPIST

If you believe your child would benefit from therapeutic services, consider the following when choosing a play therapist.

Find a provider: Start by searching the website for the Association for Play Therapy (A4PT.org) to find providers listed in your area. You will find a compiled list of individuals trained in play therapy by area.

Consider location: It is important to find a provider who's located close by. Many children attend play therapy on a weekly basis. Life is already busy enough, so adding therapy into the mix can feel like an overwhelming task.

Interview the therapist: Child-therapist connection is a must for successful treatment. Trust your gut when you meet with a provider. Schedule an intake session first before bringing in your child. This will allow you to get a sense of the therapist before your child meets them. Allow your child to refuse to go back if they felt uncomfortable with the therapist. Encourage them to use their voice—this is about them!

Ask the right questions: During your initial contact with the therapist, ask as many questions as needed. Every therapist has a slightly different way of doing things. Find out what type of sessions they typically offer, length of session, frequency, and how often you will be in the room all together. If you are uncertain about anything, it's best to find out up front!

Know their skills: It is important to ask if the therapist often treats other children with the same problem as your child. You want to make sure that they have the skills to support you and your child.

Scheduling: Consistency is a key factor in your child's ability to make progress. Ensure that the provider you are considering can meet with your child on a regular basis. Treatment will typically start out as weekly, before becoming bi-weekly, and, toward the end of treatment, monthly.

Cost: Unfortunately, cost is almost always a factor in your ability to access mental health-related services. Seek out someone who can accept your insurance if you have coverage, or someone who has a fee that you are able to pay consistently.

CHAPTER TWO

Opening the Play Therapy Toolbox

In this chapter, I'll provide you with a more nuanced overview of the activities featured in chapters 3 through 9. You'll learn about the components of the activities, how I've selected them, and, most importantly, why you'd want to engage your child in them. I'll also give you some ideas on where to start, based on your child's particular needs. In sum, although you are not providing play therapy to your child, it's helpful for you to understand the therapeutic benefit of these types of play activities before you begin using them.

Harnessing the
Power of Play

As previously stated, this book is not an effective substitute for therapy. But it can help parents feel more equipped to support a child who may be struggling in some way—and to join them in fun, meaningful play. While the activities in this book may prove especially helpful for children experiencing difficulties in expressing emotions, managing behaviors, and/or dealing with trauma-related symptoms, they can really provide benefits to all children between the ages of three to nine. As the parent, you are the expert on your child: Use your judgement to experiment with which activities best meet the needs of your child.

In general, engaging your child in these types of activities can:

- Help strengthen the parent-child connection, which is the first step in changing your child's behaviors.

- Help your child better understand their internal state, and therefore more effectively identify their emotions.

- Increase your child's ability to manage their emotions—learning to accept and understand them without allowing them to take over.

- Help your child to reconnect with play. Many of the parents I work with report that their children have begun to crave time in front of a screen. This can lead to a multitude of behavioral challenges, such as a rise in tantrums, aggressive behaviors, and whining, as well as changes in impulse control and even sleep patterns. The activities in this book are a great way for parents to break their child's screen dependencies.

- Improve sleep patterns in children struggling with healthy sleep habits.

- Help foster communication between parents and children.

- Strengthen your child's social skills.

- Improve problem-solving skills and impulse control.

- Help an anxious child manage their worries.

- Help your child develop a basic understanding of mindfulness and relaxation tools.

WHERE SHOULD I START?

Use this chart to help determine which activities are most relevant to your child. Although these particular chapters are a good place to start, all chapters can prove useful in helping your child reach these goals.

Goal	Activities
Increase parent-child connection	All chapters
Improve parent-child communication	Chapter 3, Chapter 5, Chapter 6
Improve problem-solving skills	Chapter 5, Chapter 6, Chapter 7
Increase impulse control	Chapter 5, Chapter 7
Decrease angry/emotional outbursts	Chapter 3, Chapter 4, Chapter 5
Decrease aggressive behaviors	Chapter 3, Chapter 5, Chapter 8, Chapter 9

Goal	Activities
Decrease anxiety symptoms	Chapter 3, Chapter 6, Chapter 9
Improve sleep	Chapter 8, Chapter 9
Improve child's ability to understand and describe emotions	Chapter 3, Chapter 4, Chapter 5, Chapter 9
Decrease screen dependency	All chapters
Increase child's self-esteem	Chapter 3, Chapter 4, Chapter 6, Chapter 7
Develop child's awareness of internal state (e.g., reading body cues for information)	Chapter 4, Chapter 9

About the Activities

A good play therapist will continually collect new techniques over the course of their career, deploying different strategies to meet the evolving needs of different clients. For my own practice, I have spent years attending trainings, taking classes, obtaining guidance from others in the field, and poring through hundreds of books, articles, and magazines related to the treatment of children. Although I've become an expert in play therapy, I've found that some of my favorite and most powerful techniques were developed on a whim, in the midst of a session, often invented by my clients themselves during the therapeutic process. Suffice it to say: the play therapy toolbox is bottomless.

Yet no matter where the tools in this book come from, all of them share one thing in common: they are rooted in a child-centered framework. This means that they put the child at the center of everything. When children are engaged in a relationship that is equal, they gain a sense of power they often don't feel in other situations. This is a unique component of the therapeutic relationship, which often allows children to feel free enough to meet their own needs in the moment.

Since you're acting not as a therapist but a parent, the activities in this book are—among many other things—intended to strengthen and shape the parent-child bond. This bond is the framework for how your child sees and experiences the world. Due to its joyful nature, play inherently creates the space for healthy connections to flourish with others as well. When children are able to forge these connections, they're more capable of managing, regulating, and engaging with their environment.

EACH ACTIVITY IN THE BOOK HAS THE FOLLOWING ELEMENTS...

A **Description** to help you understand the activity's benefit(s) for your child, and how it can help fulfill said benefit(s).

A list of **Materials** needed for the given activity. (This book assumes you have a pen or pencil on hand.)

Step-by-step **Instructions**, designed to walk you through how to do the activity—and how best to engage your child in it. As the expert on your child, it is okay for you to take liberties with these directions to best meet the needs of your child and family.

A **Play Tip**, where you'll find a recommendation for more effectively engaging a struggling child and/or a playful strategy to heighten imagination or connection.

Naturally, not every activity will be relevant or appropriate for every child.

STOCK YOUR PLAYROOM

Many of the activities in this book require nothing more than a playful parent-child connection. Additionally, almost every child I've worked with in a professional setting, or engaged with in a personal setting, has had the ability to make almost any item into a toy. You'll notice that the imaginative nature most children possess is present in many of these activities.

That said, some of the activities require materials to better engage the child—ranging from household items, to basic art materials, to simple toys, such as dolls, dress-up clothes, and play doctor kits.

Here is a comprehensive list of materials used in this book:

- Pillows
- Blankets
- Cotton balls
- Laundry basket
- Blank paper
- Paint
- Markers
- Colored pencils
- Crayons
- Small whiteboard

- Tiny treasures (rubber bands, googly eyes, beads, rocks and pebbles, shells, plastic straws, buttons, pom-poms, foam shapes, leaves, string, toothpicks, cocktail umbrellas, mini erasers)
- Dice
- Play doctor's kit

- Play microphone
- Play kitchen food and accessories
- Bubbles
- Animal figurines
- Stuffed animals
- Bubble gum
- Tissue box
- Paper towel roll
- Art smock
- Tablecloth

On-the-Page Activities

Some of the activities in this book, like those that are art-based, provide the space you and your child need to imagine and create right here in the book itself. One example is the activity "How Does It Smell?" (page 84). This activity takes children on an adventure through your home and is designed to help facilitate your child's connection to their sense of smell. During this activity, there will be space for you and your child to notice what you smell and track it on the page of the book itself. Another example is Dream Catcher (page 50), which is designed to help your child manage worries about nightmares. This activity gives your child a template in which they can create and color their own dream catcher. Of course, should you want or need more space, you can start with the book's pages and use additional pieces of paper as needed.

Off-the-Page Activities

The majority of the activities in this book will occur off the page. For these activities, your child won't write or create anything on the activity page of the book itself; rather, these activities will engage you and your child in movement around your house; playful imagination; or calm, soothing exercises. One example of this type of activity is a simple game of Follow the Leader (page 72). Another example of this type of activity is Lava Floor (see page 79), in which you and your child use your imagination and creativity to chart a course through your house, as if it were a jungle, the floor of which is covered in lava. During these kinds of activities, you and your child will delight in the playful nature of connection, movement, and creativity together.

Some other off-the-page activities encourage you to challenge your child to follow limits or explore the impact of change in the moment. Red Light, Green Light (see page 118) is another classic child's game, which you can use here to help your child deal with impulse control. Furthermore, the outdoor activities in chapter 8 and the guided relaxation techniques in chapter 9 can help your child learn to develop a connection to their internal state of being—how they're feeling both emotionally and physically.

PLAY BY THESE RULES

1. **No phones.** During these activities, it is important to limit distractions. Screen time and cell phone use decrease joyful, playful engagement. As parents, it is vital to model a healthy presence and engagement with your child.

2. **Practice joyful, playful engagement.** For something to be playful, it should elicit joy. Try to allow this time to be lighthearted and silly.

3. **Let them lead.** Work to limit micromanaging your child, allowing them to take the lead during these activities. If they want to change the rules of the activity or do it in a different way, that's okay. Play sparks creativity, and some of the best games and activities come from moments like this.

4. **Notice out loud.** When you are fully present and playing with your child, practice verbalizing your observations—of their facial expressions, how they're moving their body, and more. Doing so will send the message to your child that you are fully present and engaged in the play with them.

5. **Minimal redirection.** Setting limits are important, especially for safety, but if your child doesn't want to do a specific activity or doesn't feel ready to do it at that moment, forcing them with constant redirection or corrections won't help. This will increase frustration for all involved.

6. **Safety first.** A key component of healthy, positive engagement is safety. If we feel safe, we can connect with the people around us. Consider how to continue to make your child feel both physically and emotionally safe while using this book.

7. **Stay calm.** Healthy playful connection can't occur if you as the parent are getting overwhelmed. An agitated or angry parent cannot calm or de-escalate an out-of-control child. If your child's behaviors need to be redirected to ensure that you are regulating your own emotions, it is okay to take a moment like this to walk away, take deep breaths, or even say, "I am having a hard time, and I need to calm down so I can help you calm down."

CHAPTER THREE

Connection Activities

Children learn how to interpret the world around them based on their early relationships with parents and caregivers. In *I Love You Rituals*, developmental psychologist Becky Bailey observes that our attachment, or connection, to these figures within the first few years of life creates an internal road map that guides us on our journey through life, shaping the way we experience everything from competition, to friendships, to romantic partnerships.

Though most of the activities in this book support and strengthen the parent-child connection, this chapter has a particular emphasis on that most vital bond. If you notice that the connection with your child continues to feel strained, impacting your ability to connect with them or their ability to seek support from you, it is imperative to seek additional professional support. Play therapy is a powerful tool to help foster and strengthen the parent-child relationship!

Many of the activities in this chapter, and several others throughout the book, are based on or inspired by a specific play therapy technique, termed Theraplay. Developed in the 1960s to help foster and strengthen the attachment bond between a parent and child, Theraplay, according to *Parenting With Theraplay*, necessitates that parents and children connect in a playful manner throughout the entire therapeutic process. These activities are intended to help children feel better about themselves through the parent's level of engagement, connection, and nurture, making them more confident and well-regulated in turn.

For the purposes of this book, I have taken these concepts and made them accessible for parents and children to engage in together, without the support or guidance of a therapist.

Snuggle Time

The goal of this activity is to boost your child's positive mood. When we experience healthy, safe touch, our body receives a big dose of oxytocin, a hormone that engenders feelings of love and connection. The more frequently we are able to hold our child in a safe and nurturing way, the more we will be connected with them.

1. Start by having your child sit in your lap.

2. Next, wrap your arms around them tight while you sing the snuggle song (to the tune of "London Bridge"):

   > Snuggle safely in my arms
   > In my arms, in my arms
   > I love it when you snuggle tight
   > In my arms

3. As you hold your child, sing to and snuggle them, gently swaying your child just like you did when they were a baby!

Play Tip: This game is great to play right before bed. Lay in your child's bed and hold them tightly while you sing them the snuggle song!

Laughing Popcorn

Feeding our child is one of the first ways we connect with them. In the early stages of development, feeding and food are directly tied to love and nurture. I've adapted this feeding game from its more therapeutic version to best engage your child in a more age-appropriate, food-based connection activity.

MATERIALS: Popcorn

1. Start by popping some delicious popcorn. Choose a type of popcorn you feel comfortable with your child eating a healthy portion of.

2. Sit across from each other with the bowl of popcorn in the middle. Decide who is going to be the "laugher" and who is going to be the "echo."

3. If you are the laugher, try to make the silliest laugh you can think of. If you are the echo, try your best to copy the silly laugh.

4. After the echo repeats the silly laugh, they should wait for the laugher to stop laughing (to make sure they don't choke) and place a piece of popcorn into the mouth of the laugher.

5. Take turns being the laugher and the echo, making sure to always place a piece of popcorn in the mouth of the other player.

Play Tip: It is imperative to note that with any game that involves feeding, the food must not be used as a bargaining chip for good behaviors. Your child must *always* get the piece of popcorn after their turn. Remember: feeding is connected to love. Withholding food during this type of connection game will not create a sense of love, laughter, and connection!

Blanket Fort Snuggle

Touch is a key aspect of healthy human development—we all need physical connection to survive. Anytime we are able to turn simple play into a special connection, we increase our child's feelings of self-worth. This activity helps to foster this connection in a fun way.

MATERIALS: Chairs, blankets, pillows, stuffed animals, your child's favorite book

1. Start by engaging your child in the fun and imaginative task of building a blanket fort.

2. Use chairs as the sides, draping blankets across the top to create a roof.

3. Fill the interior with pillows, more blankets, and your child's favorite stuffed animals.

4. Grab your child's favorite book.

5. Snuggle up inside the fort reading together!

Play Tip: If you are able to turn off the lights, add flashlights to your fort. Make it feel like you are on a camping adventure in your own home!

Highs and Lows

The goal of this activity is to help you and your child engage in a conversation about their day. Some parents find that when they ask their child how their day was (say, after school), they get simple, short, one-word answers. Framing your question by asking your child to identify both a positive and negative aspect of their day opens the conversation up and can yield a more fruitful dialogue.

1. Start by asking your child to share a high point of their day. If they're stuck, give them suggestions, such as:

    a. A moment they felt excited.
    b. A moment they accomplished something they were struggling with.
    c. A delicious food they really enjoyed.

2. After your child shares their high point, reflect back what you heard them saying by noticing how that must have felt for them, such as: *It must have been so exciting to play chase in gym class today!*

3. Next, ask your child to share a low point of their day. If they're stuck, give them suggestions, such as:

    a. A moment they felt overwhelmed by a task.
    b. A moment they felt out of control.
    c. A moment their feelings were hurt.

4. After your child shares their low, reflect back what you hear them saying by noticing how that might have felt for them, such as: *It must have been hard to understand when your friend decided to pick someone else as their partner instead of you.*

Play Tip: This is a perfect activity to play in the car on the way home from school. Another great time to engage your child in this type of connection is right before bed, as a way to reflect on the day.

Secret Handshake

The goal of this activity is to strengthen parent-child connection through the creation of a secret, special handshake. Having something that only the two of you know about and can do daily will help your child to feel noticed, special, and connected to you.

1. Engage your child in making up a secret handshake together.
2. Take turns adding in different gestures, like high fives, hand clasps, and finger wiggles.
3. Make the handshake long enough that it feels unique and important, but short enough that you can remember it!

Play Tip: Do this secret handshake before your child has to make a transition, like going to school for the day or going to bed for the night.

Hide-and-Seek

I probably don't have to tell you what Hide-and-Seek is, or how to play! It's a classic game that many children love. But it can also help strengthen the parent-child bond in a specific way: through this game, children learn that even if you can't see each other, their parent will always be there for a joyful reunion!

1. Start the game by deciding who will be hiding and who will be seeking. In these types of games, it is best to let your child lead, allowing them to decide who is hiding and who is seeking first.

2. The person seeking will count to 10 while the other player hides.

3. Once you reach 10, say out loud, *Ready or not, here I come!*

4. As you search for your child, track your excitement to find them: *I am looking in the living room now, I hope you're in here! I can't wait to give you a big hug when I find you!*

5. Once you find your child, express extreme joy in the reunion, as if you haven't seen them in a long time: *Oh my, I am so happy to see you again! I knew I would find you. I love when we are together!*

Play Tip: Depending on the age of your child, try to hide in more obvious places. The goal of this game is to experience the joy of coming back together. You don't want your child to be too overwhelmed by the task of trying to find you!

Magic Face Paint

I adapted this activity from a Theraplay intervention frequently used with families. It is intended to help send the message that your child is worthy of care and nurture, no matter what! When we offer nurture to our child without them asking, without any expectation that they return the nurture, we strengthen their internal feelings of self-worth.

MATERIALS: Multicolored pom-poms

1. Start by explaining to your child that you are going to use your imagination to help you paint each other's faces.

2. Decide who is going to be the artist and who is going to be the canvas first.

3. If you are the artist, you will use the magic of your imagination and the multicolored pom-poms to paint the other person's face.

4. If you are the canvas, decide what design you'd like created. Examples may include a butterfly, unicorn, superhero, or tiger. Remind your child that they have the best painting skills, because it's all pretend!

5. Use the multicolored pom-poms as your brush and softly paint the design onto the other person's face.

Play Tip: As the parent, do your best to track what you are creating, noticing out loud the colors you are using and where you are placing them. For example: *Now I am painting your butterfly wings a pretty pink color right here on your cheek!*

Snack Picture

The goal of this activity is to incorporate the excitement and creativity of creation with the nurture and connection of feeding. During this game, you and your child will use snacks to "color" in the picture on the following page. After you playfully connect together, you will delight in the silliness of feeding each other pieces of your creations.

MATERIALS: Different-colored snacks

1. Start by allowing your child to choose one of the pictures to help "color" in.

2. Hunt through your kitchen together to find different foods that have colors you would normally use to color in the picture. For example, find green foods for the dinosaur picture.

3. Have your child place different foods on the picture they choose, as if they were coloring it.

4. When they have completed "coloring" their picture, take turns feeding each other bites of the snacks you chose.

Play Tip: Do not withhold any type of snack items during games that involve feeding. Connection and love are tied to feeding, so only offer foods for the picture that you are comfortable with your child eating.

The Big Game

For this game, you'll use the play therapy technique of "tracking" to help foster and strengthen your connection to your child. Imagine that you are a sports announcer and your child is playing in the biggest game of their career. Your vocal tone during this game should be extremely enthusiastic, as if your child is the MVP and about to score the game-winning point. The more playful you are during this game, the greater the connection you'll make.

MATERIALS: Play microphone (optional)

1. You can engage in this type of talk during any type of play your child is doing. Many parents like to start with this type of engagement when their child is doing something active.

2. Hold the play microphone (if using) and start your sports announcing bit: *Mary has the ball; she is holding it in her hands. She is thinking about throwing it, but she isn't sure who to pass it to. She is taking a big deep breath, oh, and just like that, she kicks the ball to Dad! Wow, she knew just how to do that!*

3. Continue tracking your child for a few moments as they engage in play. Your vocal tone should stay playful and enthusiastic throughout.

Play Tip: Many children *love* this game! Ask your child what they would like to do while you play this game. Allow them to engage in any type of play while you track them.

"How Does Your Garden Grow?"

This game is inspired by Becky Bailey's *I Love You Rituals*. The goal of this activity is to playfully connect with your child through song and gentle touch; it also has a layer of sensory engagement through the use of finger paints.

MATERIALS: Non-toxic finger paints, face paints, and/or markers

1. Start by choosing an art material you are comfortable using on your child's skin—any type of non-toxic paint or makers will work.

2. Slowly paint a picture of a flower on your child's hand, cheek, arm, or foot. As you gently paint an image of the flower, sing to them, inserting your child's name into the song:

    > Mary, Mary, quite contrary
    > How does your garden grow?
    > With silver bells, and cockleshell
    > And little maids all in a row

Play Tip: Repeat the song a few times, drawing flowers on both of your child's hands, feet, and cheeks!

Goodnight Eyes

Some of the most important moments in your child's day are the final moments before bed. How we feel before we fall asleep can affect our sleep pattern and dreams, and impact the following day in turn. Many parents struggle with bedtime, whether due to their child's inability to sleep on their own, fear of nightmares, or defiance about going to bed. Adding a simple connection activity to your nightly routine can help increase positive engagement during this crucial time. I adapted this activity from Becky Bailey's *I Love You Rituals*, making it a bit more playful and silly.

1. Tell your child that you want say goodnight to all the parts of them, because you love every inch of them!

2. You will travel down your child's body, offering a loving goodnight to their different body parts. As you say goodnight to each body part, offer a gentle touch and massage if your child likes this type of touch.

3. Start at your child's hair with a statement, like: *Goodnight, hair. You are so curly and soft.* Then, gently pat or stroke your child's hair.

4. Move along by offering a loving goodnight to your child's eyes, ears, nose, cheeks, neck, shoulders, arms, hands, fingers, belly, legs, and feet, ending with their toes.

Play Tip: Make eye contact with the part of your child's body you are offering love to. Imagine you are looking at them with the most loving eyes you have ever had!

Cotton Ball Hide

This activity is adapted from a well-known Theraplay intervention that works to engage children in a low-key but playful game of hide-and-seek. The game is great to play when you want to create connections with your child without tons of physical movement—such as when you are working to calm your child down before bed.

MATERIALS: Cotton ball

1. Explain to your child that you are going to play a new kind of hide-and-seek.

2. Give the child a cotton ball and tell them to hide it somewhere on them. You will turn around or close your eyes.

3. After your child has hidden the cotton ball, you will search around them to find it!

Play Tip: Instead of a cotton ball, give your child a piece of candy to hide. Once the candy is found, enjoy it together, noticing how it smells and tastes!

Invisible Hurts

Most children have challenging moments with siblings, peers, and other adults, which can lead to hurt feelings that can't be seen. This activity I picked up from a colleague is intended to allow parents to strengthen their connection by offering empathy to their child's internal struggles—in particular, those they might not know how to express.

MATERIALS: Bandage

1. Ask your child how they are feeling on the inside today.

2. No matter if the response is good or bad, ask them if they have any hurts that can't be seen. Say something like, *Many of us have invisible hurts that can't be seen, like when we feel sad or disappointed. We can hurt on the inside, and sometimes no one can even tell.*

3. Offer to place a bandage anywhere on their body that will help their invisible hurts heal.

Play Tip: Help your child better express their invisible hurt by asking, *If your invisible hurt could talk, what would it want me to know?*

Memory Statue

This activity adds a level of parent-child connection to a lighthearted memory challenge. The more present we are with our children, the better they will feel about themselves. Even a game as simple as this one can help boost your child's self-esteem.

MATERIALS: Hat, scarf, dress-up clothes (all optional)

1. Start by explaining to your child how the game works.

   a. One person will be the "statue" and one person will be using their memory. If you are the statue first, you will stand still like a statue for a moment while the other person uses the pretend camera in their brain to take a picture of how you look. The person using their memory will briefly leave the room, while the statue changes something small about their appearance. Then the person will reenter the room and try to figure out what has changed on the statue!

   b. The change could be more obvious like putting on a hat, scarf, or dress-up item; or it could be less obvious, like slightly changing the way you were standing.

2. Switch roles and take turns as many times as your child likes.

Play Tip: Don't forget that the real goal is to notice your child, not to win the game! Do your best to playfully notice what has changed and what has stayed the same with a statement, such as: *Oh, good, your bright blue eyes stayed the same. Hmm . . . it must be this cape that changed!*

CHAPTER FOUR

Arts, Crafts, and Music Activities

The activities in this chapter involve painting, drawing, creative creations, and music—all of which light up the parts of our brain connected to feelings. Engaging children in this type of play helps them regulate their emotions and feel more connected to themselves and others.

Draw Your World

This activity is a great way to gather insights into how your child is currently viewing their world. It's important to remember that there is no wrong way to create this image. Children interpret their world differently depending on many factors, such as their developmental stage, family structure, temperament, and life experience.

MATERIALS: Crayons, markers, or paint

1. Instruct your child to create their world on the page. This creation could include pictures of people in their family, friends, their school, places they like to go, or things they like to do. Anything in their world can be included!

2. Make sure to let your child know that there's no wrong way to draw their world.

3. Have them color, draw, paint, or create any kind of image in the space on the following page to best describe their world.

Play Tip: If your child doesn't enjoy drawing or is critical of their drawing ability, cut out images from magazines and help them create a collage to represent their world.

Portrait View

The goal of this activity is to really understand how you and your child see each other. Perspective and viewpoint are an important part of understanding how your child might be feeling and how they perceive you—not to mention, how you perceive them.

MATERIALS: Crayons, markers, and/or pencils, whiteboard and whiteboard markers (optional)

1. Start by offering your child the coloring materials they prefer.

2. Tell them you are going to play a silly drawing game, reminding them that the goal is to try their best. If your child is extra critical of their artistic skills, encourage them by allowing them to draw first.

3. Sit across from your child, pretending they are an artist in a master class and you are the model.

4. Ask them to draw you, just as they see you, in the space on the following page or on a whiteboard (if using).

5. When they finish, intently notice all the aspects of the drawing with statements like:

    a. *I noticed how you drew my hair that color.*
    b. *I see you made my arms so long, so I can really hug you tight.*

6. After they have completed their portrait of you, offer to create a portrait of them.

7. Once complete, intently notice all the things you love about them, such as:

    a. *I drew your loving blue eyes.*
    b. *I drew the kind heart that beats inside your chest!*

Play Tip: If you have a highly active child who struggles to sit still for a lengthy activity, use a small, additional whiteboard or sheet of paper and set the timer. Draw a portrait of each other at the same time in under two minutes!

Surprise Drawing

Many children struggle with any type of change. A simple tweak in their day's routine can sometimes ruin an entire day. This activity is a silly and creative way to help children learn to deal with the unexpected. You will create a surprise drawing with your child; doing so in a calm and playful way will help them feel mastery over change and unexpected moments.

MATERIALS: Index cards, hat or bowl, drawing materials (crayons, markers, paints, and/or colored pencils)

1. Write down different items on as many index cards as you like. These will be the items that you and your child will attempt to draw together. Examples may include: a dog, window, house, apple, sky, lion, etc. Choose anything you want to try to draw together!

2. Fold the index cards in half, then place them in a hat or bowl.

3. Take turns picking the cards out of the hat. After each card is chosen, attempt to draw what's written down together on a piece of paper.

4. Try to make the complete drawing as cohesive as possible, even if these things wouldn't be in a picture together normally!

Play Tip: Try to make a silly story as you create the image about why these items are all together. Remember how important it is to laugh together during play!

Musical Instrument Creation

The goal of this activity is to create sound together. Music is a powerful healing tool that lights up the expressive areas of our brain. Whenever we are engaged in music in a playful manner, we can increase our ability to regulate our emotions. Children love to make something out of nothing, and this is a great way to do that!

MATERIALS:

Empty tissue box   Empty paper towel roll   Glue or tape

Rubber bands   Wax paper   Dry beans

1. Go around the house with your child to find the materials listed above that they'll need to make a guitar and maracas.

2. Wrap the rubber bands around the empty tissue box. Make sure they are wrapped around the opening; this will make a musical sound when they are strummed or plucked, similar to a guitar.

3. Cover the end of an empty paper towel roll with waxed paper, attaching it with glue or tape. Fill it with the dry beans. Then cover the other end. Give it a shake to test the sound!

Play Tip: Create a family band! Make as many instruments as members in your family, and create a silly song about your family using your instruments.

Smell-Good Playdough

Many parents tell me they find that their child is often daydreaming or easily distracted. Engaging your child's senses, especially their sense of smell, can be extremely grounding, and helps them focus. In this activity, you'll create a strong, positive sensory experience through the use of this delightful-smelling homemade playdough recipe.

MATERIALS:

2 cups all-purpose flour

½ cup salt

2 tablespoons cream of tartar

1½ cups water

Food coloring, as needed

10 to 15 drops essential oil of your choice

2 tablespoons cooking oil

1. In a large bowl, mix together the flour, salt, and cream of tartar.

2. In a saucepan, add the water, mixing in the food coloring until desired color is achieved. Then, mix in the essential oil and cooking oil.

3. Add the dry ingredient mixture to the saucepan, stirring well.

4. Cook over low to medium heat until the dough starts to form, stirring as needed. Once formed and dry, remove dough from heat and let cool.

5. Knead for 3 to 5 minutes, or until dough is smooth and squishy.

6. Engage your child in the playful expression possible with playdough. Create playful animals, snowmen, or even your favorite "recipe."

Play Tip: Have your child cook the dough with you! Teaching your child the simple steps involved in this recipe helps build confidence through independence.

One-Minute Drawing

I learned this activity from a colleague who attended a conference with play therapist Dr. Terry Kottman, founder of The Encouragement Zone. In my own practice, I use this activity as a way to communicate about a difficult situation a child has experienced when they are unwilling to talk about it. During the one minute, your child will draw a picture of some kind. The speed relieves the pressure of having to talk about something difficult for long. This can open the lines of communication, whether about how their day is going or about a problem they might be having.

MATERIALS: Timer, whiteboard, and whiteboard markers (optional)

1. Explain to your child that they are going to do a drawing that describes their day, but that they only have one minute to do it. (Use a paper and pencil if you don't have a whiteboard.) Prompt your child to draw with questions like:

    a. *Draw for me in one minute a picture of your favorite part of your day.*
    b. *Draw for me in one minute a moment today when you had a big feeling.*
    c. *Draw for me in one minute a picture of what it was like during lunch today.*

2. Remind them that *no one* is a good artist in only one minute.

3. Announce that you're starting the timer. Count down the last five seconds.

4. After your child completes their drawing, switch places.

Play Tip: If you have more than one whiteboard, engage more members of the family! Share your creations when the time runs out.

Dream Catcher

Many parents report that their child struggles to sleep well as a result of nightmares, sleep regression, life changes, and other factors. Helping your child create a dream catcher to use as a tool to catch bad dreams is a wonderful way to help them deal with sleep-related anxiety.

MATERIALS: Drawing materials (crayons, markers, paints, and/or colored pencils)

1. Before you start your child's bedtime routine, tell them you are going to help them have good dreams.

2. Explain that dreams are just our brain's way of figuring out our day, and that they are not real and can't hurt us.

3. Have your child color in the dream catcher on the following page, while you recount the story of the dream catcher (adapted from DreamCatcher.com):

   > A native tribe believed that everybody dreams. We all have good dreams and bad dreams. Our dreams float through the air and find us. This dream catcher will work like a dream filter. It will notice if you have a bad dream coming and help you sleep peacefully.

4. As your child colors the page, have them think of all the wonderful parts of their day that they hope to have dreams about!

Play Tip: If your child is really struggling with sleep, hang this above their bed. Take turns telling the dream catcher what type of dreams you both would want to have that night as part of the bedtime routine.

Worry Jar

Worry and anxiety are normal parts of life. Yet some children, like some adults, can be consumed by these emotions. Worries can range from big fears, like accidents at school, to minor concerns, like walking into a dark room alone. Creating a worry jar with your child is a great way to help them understand that everyone has worries—and to ultimately help them contain or overcome them.

MATERIALS: Jar with a lid, colored paper, markers

1. Explain that you are going to create a family worry jar. If possible, allow all members of the family to decorate the jar together.

2. Cut the colored paper into strips.

3. Instruct your child to write down different worries on the paper strips and place them in the jar. Don't force your child to share their worries unless they want to.

4. As the parent, it is important to also share honest, age-appropriate worries with your child. This will normalize the experience of having a worry. For example: *I feel worried when the weatherman says it is icy on the roads and we have to go somewhere, even though I know that I can drive the car slow to keep us safe.*

5. As each worry is written out, trap it in the jar! Remind your child that the worry will be trapped in the jar, so they don't have to think about it anymore.

Play Tip: Keep the worry jar in a central location with paper available at all times. When you notice a moment of worry arise, have your child write down the worry and place it in the jar for safekeeping.

"What a Brave Child You Are!"

The goal of this activity is to offer love and admiration for your child. Showing love to your child through song is another developmentally appropriate way to create connection, as singing tends to be one of first ways we communicate with our children (think: lullabies). This playful take on a classic song is inspired by Becky Bailey's *I Love You Rituals* and is commonly used during Theraplay (see page 24 for more info). When I became a parent, I started singing this to my daughter, tweaking the words a bit to better fit the needs of our relationship.

1. Snuggle up with your child, gazing into their eyes, and sing this song (to the tune of "Twinkle, Twinkle, Little Star"):

   > Twinkle, twinkle little star, what a BRAVE child you are!
   > With soft brown hair and nice round cheeks, and big brown
   > eyes from which you peek.
   > Twinkle, twinkle, little star, what a BRAVE child you are!

2. Adjust the words of the song to describe your child's hair color and eye color.

Play Tip: Sing the song anytime your child needs a confidence boost. Pick different adjectives that best suit your child, such as wonderful, funny, smart, talented, etc.

Challenge Song

One way to help your child overcome a challenging situation is to match the moment with a song. Short, little songs used in challenging moments can make the moment exciting and playful, and increase your child's ability to stay regulated during a stressful time.

This idea was actually inspired by my own childhood. My mother would often sing little songs during transition times or challenging moments. For example, she made a little tune about going potty before we left the house. Naturally, I don't remember much about my potty-training days, but I do remember the joyful feelings I felt every time my mother would sing me this song. She would often sing it in the few minutes before we left the house, when she would attempt to get my sister and me to use the potty just one more time.

1. Start by thinking of a transition moment that is often a struggle for you as a parent. For example, the moment when you are rushing to get your child's coat and shoes on before the bus comes.

2. Before you allow this moment to become overwhelming for both you and your child, offer the direction clearly first. For example: *Maria, I need you to put your coat on.*

3. Next, shift into a more playful tone, singing the next steps. For example (to the tune of "The More We Get Together"):

    > We are putting on our coats, our coats, our coats.
    > We're putting on shoes to get to the bus.

4. Pass the song to your child using a stage whisper, prompting them to sing next: *What should be the next line of the song? Can you sing it?*

5. Take turns making up songs about putting on your child's coat and shoes, finding their backpack, and so on.

Play Tip: Keep your directions clear from the start so your child knows you still need them to complete the task, while turning the transition or challenging moment into a musical experience, thereby changing the moment from one of stress to one of joy.

Mirror Message

Our children are often confronted with negative messages about themselves. Whether these messages are from peers, the media, or the byproduct of challenging experiences, it can be hard at times for our children to believe they are good enough. Sometimes, in the midst of an overwhelming week, we can forget to stop and remind our children of the amazing qualities they have. A mirror message is a fun way to tell your child all the things about them that you admire and love.

MATERIALS: White crayon, watercolors

1. Using a white crayon, write down on the space provided on the following page the things you love most about your child. They can include words and phrases, such as caring, funny, smart, a good big brother, and so on. Fill the page with as many qualities and attributes as you can think of!

2. After you've finished writing, encourage your child to paint freely with the watercolors all over the mirror page.

3. The watercolors will uncover your secret message. As the words become clear, look at your child as you read them the message. Engaging your child in this type of activity will bring to light their many good qualities.

Play Tip: For added admiration, remind your child of a time when they demonstrated one of the qualities you wrote down. For example: *I know you are a good big brother because you helped teach your little brother how to shoot hoops!*

Felt Feelings Faces

Teaching our child that emotions are a normal part of life and necessitates openly talking about how we feel. When we avoid our emotions, it can lead children to believe they should be ashamed of their feelings, creating a polarized view of something fundamental to the human experience. The goal of this activity is to engage in playful feelings exploration. It involves parents sharing how they're feeling—make sure to be honest, but age-appropriate!

MATERIALS: Felt (various colors), scissors

1. Engage your child in cutting out different felt shapes that could represent how our faces look when we feel different feelings.

2. Cut out happy eyes, angry eyes, and the like. Also create eyebrows, mouths, hair—anything else that will help bring alive the face's emotional expressions. If you and your child struggle to create expressions out of felt, make different emotional expressions at each other as a guide for eyes, mouth, and eyebrow shapes.

3. Take turns creating the different emotional expressions in the face circle on the following page.

4. As you make the faces, explain what emotion the face is showing and share a time when you or someone you know felt that way: *I am making a mad face. I felt mad yesterday when I burned our dinner. I was working really hard to make a yummy meal, and it all went wrong. That made me feel mad.*

Play Tip: Add an element of surprise and challenge by taking turns making a felt face without showing each other or revealing the emotions. Upon seeing the face, see if you can guess what feeling the felt is showing.

Make Your Own Puppet

This activity is an imaginative way to engage your child in storytelling, creation, and play. Puppets are frequently used during play therapy as a way to allow children to feel a separation between themselves and big feelings or problems; when a child is able to place their feelings onto the puppet instead of themselves, they are more capable of overcoming the challenge associated with them. You can use puppets with your child to have a conversation, tell a story, or even put on a show together. The playful ways to use puppets with your child are endless!

MATERIALS: Paper lunch bags, craft materials (markers, crayons, yarn, googly eyes, sequins, and the like)

1. Using the paper bags as your canvas, make different faces and characters. Create as many puppets as you would like!

2. Place your hand inside the bag, using the bottom flap of the bag to create a mouth for your puppet.

3. Use the created puppet for silly engagement, storytelling, or song creation purposes.

Play Tip: If you have a child that struggles to share things with you, try to ask about their day through puppet play! Having your puppet talk to their puppet about how they feel or what they are thinking is a great way to engage children playfully.

Stormy Boat Ride

The goal of this activity, which I adapted from Becky Bailey's *I Love You Rituals*, is to remind your child how safe and secure your relationship is. Sometimes, when a family experiences a challenging situation, children can learn to believe things about themselves that aren't true. They may believe they aren't safe, or lovable, even when this is not at all true! When we can send a message of safety and security through play, it helps to mitigate those kinds of insecurities.

MATERIALS: Dress-up clothes (optional), laundry basket or big box (optional), blankets, pillows

1. Start by creating a make-believe boat. This can be done with a laundry basket, big box, or even just your lap (the child will sit in your lap, pretending you are the boat).

2. Fill the boat with blankets and pillows to make it comfortable.

3. Tell your child that you're going to go for a boat ride, but to remember that no matter how stormy the waters get, you will keep them safe!

4. Shake, sway, and wiggle the pretend boat to mimic moving through the water in a gentle, rhythmic way. As you move the boat, start to sing:

    > Row, row, row your boat
    > Gently down the stream,
    > Merrily, merrily, merrily, merrily
    > Life is but a dream

Continued...

Stormy Boat Ride Continued...

5. Let that child know that a storm is coming: *Oh no, I see rough waters up ahead, a storm is coming! Let me hold you nice and tight, that way I can keep you safe!* Start to sing, again, this time in a manner reflective of the storm.

6. After you finish singing, let the child know the storm has passed and you are safe now: *Phew, the storm has cleared. We're now entering into gentle waters. I'd never let anything happen to you!*

7. Sing the song one more time, returning to a calm, gentle tone.

Play Tip: Add to the playful nature of this game by including dress-up clothes. Put on sailor hats or pirate clothes if your child is willing!

Feelings Playlist

Music is a natural way of expression for many people. I have found that, for slightly older children, using this type of activity helps them express their emotions in a safe and natural way.

1. Start by explaining to your child that you are going to be telling each other about the different emotions you had throughout the day in a different kind of way.

2. Instead of using words, direct your child to create a playlist of songs that describes how they felt at different times during the day. (Spotify or Apple Music works well, although you could also use YouTube or other web-based platforms.)

3. As your child creates a playlist, do the same by finding songs that express how you felt throughout your day.

4. Take turns playing each other your song selections.

Play Tip: Notice out loud how the song makes you feel. If you are listening to a fun, light-hearted song, you could reflect the joyful feeling it gives you. If you are listening to an intense song, you could reflect the angry feeling it gives you.

Feelings Drawing

Emotions are a normal part of life: we all feel mad, sad, worried, and guilty. Being able to manage your emotions doesn't mean you won't have emotions; it means you can notice how you feel and decide how to respond. This activity can help your child identify how they feel and normalize whatever it is they're feeling, in a playful and expressive way.

MATERIALS: Drawing materials (crayons, markers, paints, and/or colored pencils)

1. Start by explaining to your child that we all have feelings. One way to help understand how we feel is to check inside by noticing what our body is feeling, and by listening to what we are thinking.

2. Help them check inside right now by asking them some questions like:

   a. *How does your belly feel right now?*
   b. *What are the thoughts in your head when you think about going to [insert name of activity] alone?*
   c. *Do you notice a good feeling in your heart or a mixed-up feeling in your heart?*

3. Allow them to express what they are feeling right on the page that follows. The fewer directions the better—just let them color and create what they notice on the inside!

Play Tip: Use this as a way to help your child learn to check in with their emotions regularly. This activity is great to do after school. The more time children take to check in with how they feel, the more naturally they will be able to notice their emotions.

Handy Feelings Chart

The goal of this activity is to help your child talk about their emotions. Although many therapists focus on emotion-based work, this is also something that many parents can and should be doing with their children! This playful, art-based activity will help your child creatively connect with and express their emotions.

MATERIALS: Paper, non-toxic paint, markers, googly eyes (optional)

1. Start by explaining that you and your child are going to be creating an emotion chart.

2. Allow your child to first decide what emotions they want to chart about, for example: happy, sad, worried, mad, nervous, excited, joyful, loved, lonely, and guilty.

3. Next, let your child pick a different-colored paint to match with each emotion, for example: red for "mad" and yellow for "happy." Allow your child to be creative with their color choice; this is about how they see their emotions related to colors, not how others think they should.

4. Help your child paint the palm of their hand with one color at a time and stamp it on the paper, making different-colored handprints on the page. Write the emotion that corresponded with each color under your child's handprint.

5. After the paint dries, have your child use their handprints as the basis for their emotion faces. Use markers and googly eyes (if using) to draw on their handprint what their face would look like if they felt that way.

6. As they create the faces, talk about the emotion and different things that make you both feel that way. It is okay to share real things that make you feel emotions, as long as they are honest and age-appropriate! For example: *I feel worried when I hear about someone I love getting hurt.*

Play Tip: Hang your child's feelings chart in a common space in your home. Ask them to do a daily check-in, letting them point to which feelings they felt that day in the morning and before bed.

Body Tunes

Often our bodies react to a situation before we can identify the feeling to match. For example, some kids will go to bed the night before a big test with a stomachache, not realizing it could be caused by the nerves they feel about the test. This activity is designed to help your child understand how our bodies send different internal messages when we feel different feelings—which is a crucial element of emotional regulation.

MATERIALS: Music, crayons

1. Start by creating a playlist that your child will listen to during the activity.

2. Pick three songs with three different tempos/moods. For example:

    a. One upbeat, happy song, like "Some Things Never Change" from *Frozen II*.
    b. One angry, more intense song, like "Be Prepared" from *The Lion King*.
    c. One sad and slow song, like "When She Loved Me" from *Toy Story 2*.

3. Explain to your child that you are going to notice how their body feels when they listen to the different songs.

4. While you listen to each song, have your child color in the body outline on the following page to show the feelings inside their body. Have them use different colors to show how they are feeling in the different parts of their body.

5. After you listen to all three songs, encourage your child to notice the different ways the songs made their body feel.

Play Tip: Have your child try to name the different emotions that each song made them feel, using words such as worried, mad, sad, happy, excited, and so on.

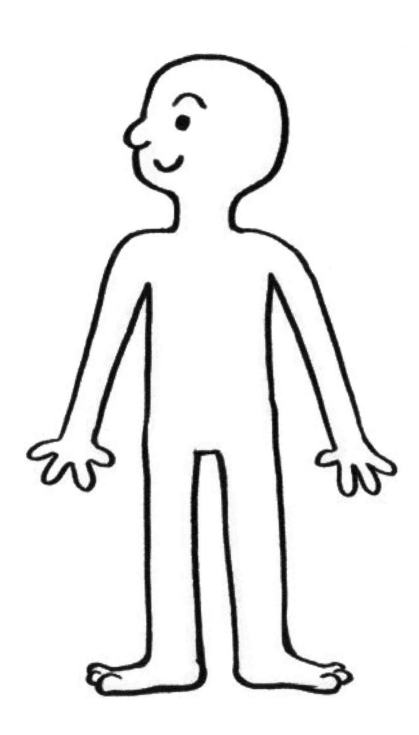

CHAPTER FIVE

Movement and Sensory Play

The activities in this chapter are designed to help children activate and explore their senses and nervous system, which plays a key role in our ability to regulate our emotions. When a child can engage their nervous system in the type of movement it needs, many parents find that the child can regulate their emotions more effectively, connect better with others, and stay present in their environment.

Follow the Leader

Attuning to your child—meeting their needs in a calm, connected manner—is an important part of creating a healthy parent-child relationship. It's also key for the development of a healthy nervous system, which leads to increased emotional regulation. Engaging in a silly game of follow the leader is a great way to boost this type of connection.

MATERIALS: Stuffed animal (optional)

1. Take turns with your child being the leader.

2. If you are the leader, you can guide your child through silly movements, dance, song, or even on an adventure through your home or backyard.

3. Allow your child to take the lead as much as possible, setting the limit: *I will keep following your lead as long as we stay safe or until you are ready to switch!*

4. If you are the one following, notice out loud what your child is asking you to do: *Oh, right now, we are doing a fun, silly dance!*

Play Tip: Bring a stuffed animal along for the game and have them also mimic the leader!

Push-Up Contest

It's not uncommon for parents to report that their children are playing in an aggressive way. Pushing and shoving, even playfully, can be a sign that your child needs to activate their nervous system in this type of movement, but in a safe, respectful way. Suggesting a playful push-up contest is a fun way to give your child's body a powerful dose of physical activity and can be grounding for an overwhelmed child.

1. Tell your child that you are going to have a playful push-up contest, where the goal is to try to do more push-ups than the other person.

2. Offer physical modifications for yourself or your child if needed, such as placing your knees on the ground.

3. Count out loud as you try your best to outlast each other.

4. Keep a scorecard. Play this game over the course of a week and encourage your child to see how many more push-ups they can do each time.

5. Let your child win. Moments of mastery are an added self-esteem boost!

Play Tip: Play sports-themed music to really increase the silliness factor (think: "Eye of the Tiger").

Body Investigator

This goal of this activity is to teach your child how to understand their physical sensations. Since our physical sensations are connected to our emotions, helping children develop this connection and understand it will only strengthen their understanding of their feelings. The body investigator is a playful way to get an answer to the question, "How does this make you feel?"

MATERIALS: Drawing materials (crayons, markers, paints, and/or colored pencils), magnifying glass (optional)

1. First, tell your child the story of the body investigator (feel free to tweak as needed):

   > Every one of us has a teeny tiny body investigator that lives inside of us. This investigator has an extremely important job. Their job is to help us figure out how our bodies feel. Our bodies have sensations that tell us how we feel, like when we feel cold, hot, or hungry. We also have sensations that happen when we have emotions, like when we get mad, we might get sweaty. We can ask our body investigator to help us understand how our body feels, so we know what we need.

2. After your child has been introduced to the idea, engage them in the body investigator game: pick a silly movement (run in place, wiggle your arms, have a dance party, spin around in a circle, etc.) and do it together.

3. After a few minutes, stop and do a body check! Tell your child to ask their body investigator how their body feels, with questions like: *Mr. Body Investigator, can you tell me how my right arm feels?*

4. Using the drawing materials, instruct your child to color in the body outline below where they notice their different body sensations. For example, after they notice how their belly feels, have them pick a color that best describes this sensation and use it to color their belly inside the body outline.

5. After they notice how one movement makes them feel, change the movement and do it, again!

Play Tip: Use a magnifying glass for an extra component of play. Have your child use it to search for their investigator, so they can figure out how their body feels!

Body Interview

Similar to Body Investigator (see page 74), this activity promotes your child's ability to connect to their body, helping them learn to listen to what their body needs and work to address those needs. Teaching this skill in a playful manner helps your child better understand it.

MATERIALS: A play microphone (optional)

1. Tell your child you are going to conduct a body interview to learn about how their body feels.

2. Start the interview questions, speaking into the play microphone (if using): *Hello Mr. Belly, this is [your child's name]'s Mom. I am curious about how you feel today?*

3. Ask silly interview questions, moving to different parts of your child's body, like their eyes, ears, mouth, nose, arms, legs, toes, elbows, and feet.

4. Ask additional questions, such as:

    a. *How do you feel today?*
    b. *What do you need right now?*
    c. *Can I give you a hug or a kiss?*
    d. *What body part should I interview next?*

Play Tip: The goal of this game is to laugh; point the microphone at the different parts of the body as if you are asking them directly. Use a silly interview voice to promote playfulness.

Cooking Time

One amazing way to engage your child's senses is by spending time together in the kitchen. Cooking together is filled with so many different opportunities for connection, challenge, problem-solving, and learning. In addition, children can practice engaging their five senses throughout the process.

MATERIALS: A simple recipe, cooking supplies

1. Ask your child to help you pick out a delicious recipe. I suggest picking something you know they can help with during most of the steps, like chocolate chip cookies, muffins, or banana bread! Consider choosing one of your child's favorite homemade snacks.

2. Start by reading the recipe together. Ask your child to help you check the kitchen to make sure you have all the ingredients you need.

3. Next, take out all the utensils needed, and take your time with the cooking. Connection is created in these simple, slow, playful interactions.

4. Let you child pour the ingredients, crack the eggs, stir the batter, mash the bananas, play with the flour—whatever they can do safely. It's okay to get messy!

5. When the food is ready, sit down and enjoy your creation together, noticing out loud how yummy it tastes.

Play Tip: Engage your child's five sense throughout, asking them sense basic questions like:
> *How does the flour feel in your hands?*
> *What does the batter smell like?*
> *What do you see happening in the oven?*

Treasure Time

The goal of Treasure Time, which I've adapted from the parenting blog *Picklebums*, is to spark creativity through unstructured play. In this activity, your child is given a collection of small items that have no specific purpose—anything a child would consider a tiny treasure. Allowing them to create something out of nothing is one of the most magical parts of play.

MATERIALS:

Any container with several compartments

Any or all of the following:

Rubber bands

Googly eyes

Beads

Rocks and pebbles

Shells

Plastic straws

Buttons

Pom-poms

Foam shapes

Leaves

String

Toothpicks

Cocktail umbrellas

Mini erasers

Scoops

Tongs

Tweezers

Blocks

Figurines

Toy cars

1. Compile as many "tiny treasures" as you can.

2. Separate these treasures by category, organizing them into your container with various compartments (Tupperware, or even an empty ice cube tray, would work here).

3. Place the tiny treasures on the table and invite your child to play with the treasures in any way that they like.

4. This play should have no limits other than safety; less guidance is more during this type of open play!

Play Tip: Take this opportunity to engage your own sense of creativity and playfulness!

Lava Floor

Daily physical movement benefits our physical health, emotional management, and overall mood. However, many children are not able to get enough physical activity throughout the day—many schools have even removed recess! When we mix creativity, movement, and connection together, as we do in this activity, we create an extremely positive experience for ourselves and our children.

MATERIALS:

Pillows

Chairs

Stepstools

Blankets

Towels

Paper

Drawing materials (crayons, markers, paints, and/or colored pencils)

1. Explain to your child that you are going to play a game they might already know! You will use your imagination to pretend the floor is hot lava and that you need to travel through the house without touching it.

2. Work with your child to build a life-size obstacle course to help you navigate through your house without touching the floor.

3. Think big and get creative: place pillows along the floor to make a path from one room to the next and use chairs and stepstools to create bridges.

4. Draw large arrows on pieces of paper and place them on the floor to help you determine which way to travel.

5. Once the course is created, see how many times you can travel along the path without touching the floor.

Play Tip: Ignite your child's imagination along the way: pretend you are in a jungle, searching for a treasure, trying to outrun the lava from a volcano.

"How Does It Sound?"

The goal of this activity is to encourage your child's connection to their auditory system. Children with auditory sensitivities often become overwhelmed in places with lots of people or loud noises. Giving children a chance to experiment with how different sounds make their bodies feel is a great way to develop a connection to the way they feel on the inside. (It may also help you determine whether your child has certain sound sensitivities.)

1. Start by telling your child you are going to engage in a sound experiment, exploring the way different sounds make them feel.

2. Take your child on a sound adventure through your home; if the weather permits, extend this experiment through your neighborhood.

3. As you and your child explore together, notice the sound of things like:

   a. The washing machine
   b. The dishwasher
   c. The water running
   d. The toilet flushing
   e. Music playing
   f. Dad's singing

4. Have your child fill out the chart provided on page 81, transcribing for them if needed.

Play Tip: Turn this into a guessing game! Have your child close their eyes and try to guess a particular sound.

What Is the Sound?	How Does It Make Me Feel? *(happy, angry, worried, annoyed, etc.)*

"How Does It Taste?"

The goal of this activity is to help your child experiment with their sense of taste. When children become overwhelmed with life's challenges, they look to gain control in any place they can—mealtime is often a place where they exert this control. Engaging your child in a playful eating experiment creates a connection with their sense of taste—it may even help particularly picky eaters become more adventurous!

MATERIALS: Small samples of various foods

1. Create a food plate filled with small samples of various foods. The sample plate could be filled with anything you and your child want to experiment with, so long as you provide only a small portion, as this sends the message that it is a playful experiment, not a meal. An example plate might include: one grape, one slice of cheese, one almond, one Goldfish cracker, one piece of broccoli, one piece of chocolate, and one slice of lunch meat.

2. Have your child try each food item and report on it, encouraging them to not notice simply whether they like it or not, but also the texture and taste of each item.

3. As they try the food, ask your child questions to increase their ability to notice:

    a. *Is it bumpy, rough, soft, or smooth?*
    b. *Does it melt in your mouth or do you have to bite it?*

4. After they try each food, have them fill out the chart provided on the following page, transcribing for them if needed.

Play Tip: This activity is intended to be fun and lighthearted. If your child does not want to try a food you offer, do not force them. If your child is extremely picky, let them pick out the foods and try them together!

The Food	How Does It Taste? *(good, bad, soft, hard, etc.)*

"How Does It Smell?"

The goal of this activity is to engage your child's sense of smell. Smells can be one of the most grounding tools available to our nervous system. When we smell something pleasant, it immediately sends a message to our brain, which can help us calm down and stay engaged in our environment.

MATERIALS:

Essential oils

Scented lotion

Scented candles

Dryer sheets

Hand soap

Vinegar

1. Explain to your child that you are going to do a smell experiment.

2. Make a collection of different scented items, such as those listed above.

3. Take turns smelling the different scented items. Encourage your child to notice which ones they like and which ones they don't.

4. Have your child fill out the chart provided on the following page, transcribing for them if needed.

Play Tip: Find a few smells that your child really likes, and ones that make them feel calm. Keep these items on hand; when your child is overwhelmed or checked out, offer this smell to help connect them to the present moment.

The Source of the Smell	How Does It Smell? (sweet, sour, nice, bad, strong, etc.)

"How Does It Feel?"

Our sense of touch is our largest sensory system, and as Mona Delahooke notes in *Social and Emotional Development in Early Intervention,* touch sensations are some of the first and most important sensations we feel. Sensitivity to touch can create problems for children. Many parents tell me that their child struggles with certain clothes or personal hygiene, due to the way something feels, as well as with physical affection, like hugs. The goal of this activity is to engage your child's sense of touch and help them to understand how things feel on their body.

1. Explain to your child that you are going to do a touch experiment.

2. Explore your home with your child, observing the way different surfaces feel with your hands or feet. Have them experiment with many different textures: rough, smooth, bumpy, sticky, wet, dry, and so on.

3. Have your child fill out the chart provided on the following page, transcribing if needed.

4. It may also be helpful to encourage your child to engage in different daily routines—like brushing their teeth, combing their hair, or taking a shower—and notice how they feel.

Play Tip: Take this activity on the road! Prompt your child to notice the way things feel outdoors, at the grocery store, or at the playground!

The Surface	How Does It Feel? *(good, bad, hot, cold, smooth, rough, etc.)*

Hug Challenge

"Sensory input" is a term used to describe the way our body interprets sensory information. Depending on the sensation, this input can make your child feel calm and soothed or agitated and overwhelmed. It all depends on their specific sensory needs. This activity will allow them to notice how different types of hugs agitate or soothe their body. You can use this information when you see that your child would benefit from an outside calming source.

MATERIALS: Blanket

1. Explain to your child you are going to do a hug experiment.

2. Following the chart provided on the next page, describe one hug at a time. After you explain the type of hug, ask your child to notice how they feel when they receive this type of hug.

3. Have your child complete the chart, transcribing for them if need be.

Play Tip: Allow your child to lead this hug experience. Take turns giving each other these different hugs and talking about how they make your body feel.

Place an X in the box to best describe how this hug makes you feel		Calm, happy, loved	Agitated, annoyed, angry
Bear Hug	Wrap your arms around your child and give them a tight squeeze.		
Butterfly Hug	Cross your arms across your chest, placing your right hand on your left bicep and your left hand on your right bicep. Gently tap your hands against your bicep back and forth, just like a butterfly flapping their wings. You can have your child give themselves a butterfly hug, or you can have them sit in your lap as you give them the hug. Allow your child to choose!		
Hand Hug	Place your right palm into your child's left palm, as if you were to give each other a high five. Gently wrap your thumbs around the back of each other's hand.		
Burrito Hug	Roll your child up in a big blanket as if you were going to make them into a big, child-sized burrito. Give them a big bear hug while they're in their burrito.		

Swing Time

This activity is one of the several Theraplay activities I've adapted for this book to help you spark a connection with your child. It offers your child's nervous system physical stimulation, as well as emotional security, so that both their physical and emotional needs are met. The more these needs are met, the more likely they are to learn to interpret and manage their emotional states. (Note: you'll need your partner or another adult to help you with this one!)

MATERIALS: A blanket large enough to hold a child

1. Start by laying the blanket on the floor. Ask your child to lay in the middle of the blanket.

2. Each adult should grab hold of the two corners on either side of the blanket. Start singing the song of your choosing, perhaps a lullaby you liked to sing to your child as an infant.

3. One adult will give the signal that they are ready to lift the child off the floor. Then, both adults will lift and cradle the child in the blanket.

4. The adults will swing the child in the blanket.

5. When the song is complete, they will place the child on the ground.

6. During this game, use verbal tracking to enhance the experience for your child, with statements such as: *We are ready to put you down, one, two, three, safely we put you down.* You can also track the landing to help your child know what you expect: *Okay, first we are putting your bottom on the ground, next your feet; okay, now we are going to lay your head down.*

Play Tip: Allow your child to take a turn being the swinger by placing their favorite doll or stuffed animal in the blanket and offering them love!

Color Mix-It-Up

I have found that using paints during play therapy sessions is a great way to help a child become calmer and more grounded in the present moment. Many kids can get caught up in what to create, but this activity takes the pressures of being a good artist off the table and allows them to engage in the soothing aspects of painting.

MATERIALS: Tablecloth, art smock, non-toxic washable paint, paper, paint brush

1. Start off by getting the painting space ready. Do whatever is needed to decrease your level of concern related to mess, perhaps by placing a tablecloth down and an art smock on your child.

2. Explain to your child that the goal of this activity is to see how many new colors of paint they can make by mixing together the colors they have.

3. Together, squeeze out dollops of paint onto the paper, allowing your child to choose as many colors as they like.

4. Allow your child to freely mix the paint together on the paper.

5. As your child mixes the paint, notice out loud how it feels to create freely in this way. When you notice out loud how *you* feel, your child is more likely to notice how *they* feel.

Play Tip: Allow your child to mix the paint using their hands. This is a great, playful way to engage different senses.

Dice Moves

The goal of this activity is to help your child engage in controlled movement, focusing on only moving one part of their body at a time. This is a skill that promotes internal body connection—that is, understanding what our body sensations are telling us.

I adapted this activity from the play therapy book, *2,4,6,8 This is How We Regulate*, tweaking it to ensure that you and your child could engage with it without the support of a therapist.

MATERIALS: A six-sided die

1. Explain to your child that you are going to play a body movement game, wherein each number of the die will represent a different body part. You and your child will take turns rolling the die.

2. If you are the roller, you get to decide what action to complete with the body part that corresponds to the number on the die. For example:

   a. Roll a 1: Clap your hands together; shake your hands back and forth really fast.
   b. Roll a 2: Wiggle your toes; point your toes; flex your feet.
   c. Roll a 3: Lift your right arm and reach it all the way to the sky.
   d. Roll a 4: Give yourself a hug by crossing your left arm across your body and squeezing tight.
   e. Roll a 5: Hop up and down on one leg; shake one leg while keeping the other one still.
   f. Roll a 6: Jump up and down; dance around.

3. If you did not roll the die, you must also do the movements that the die roller chooses.

Play Tip: Throughout the game, ask your child to notice how the different movements feel, using words like wiggly, shaky, tight, loose, soft, hard, sharp, hot, and cold.

The Five Senses Roll

This activity is a playful way to have your child notice their five senses. When we connect to our senses, we are more present in the moment. This can help us feel more regulated and in control. I would recommend playing this game when your child is on the verge of a tantrum, has just come home from a long day at school, or is about to start their homework.

MATERIALS: A six-sided die

1. Assign a sense to each number of the die:

    a. Roll a 1: Touch
    b. Roll a 2: Taste
    c. Roll a 3: Sight
    d. Roll a 4: Sound
    e. Roll a 5: Smell
    f. Roll a 6: Pick any sense you want

2. Instruct your child to roll the die. For whichever number the die lands on, ask your child to notice some things in their environment with the corresponding sense. For example:

    a. If they roll 3, ask them to notice something that they can see right now.
    b. If they roll 5, ask them to notice something that they can smell right now.

3. Take turns until you have engaged all five of your child's senses.

Play Tip: After you complete the game, ask your child to notice if they feel any different than they did before the activity. Ask them which senses were easy to notice and which ones were hard to notice. The more your child is aware of these small changes, the more present and connected they are to the moment.

Mirror Dance

When we combine connection with movement, we amplify the experience of such in the nervous system. The goal of this activity is to connect with your child by mirroring their movement.

1. Start by telling your child that you are going to take turns being the mirror: *If you are the mirror, copy whatever dance moves the dancer is doing. If you are the dancer, dance any way you like!*

2. Before you begin, make sure they know that all dance moves need to stay safe and appropriate.

3. Decide who is going to be the mirror first and who is going to be the dancer.

4. Together, pick out your favorite songs to dance to.

5. Play the music and play the game, switching as many times as you like!

Play Tip: This is another game that would benefit from noticing out loud what your child is doing when you are playing the mirror: *Oh look, we are spinning around! When you spin around, you give the mirror a big smile!* This will affirm to your child that you are present and engaged with them.

Water Adventure

Many parents talk to me about the calming effects bath time can have on their child. Water play is an amazing way to engage your child's senses. Creating play-based connections in the water is great for any child, but can be particularly helpful for sensory-sensitive children.

MATERIALS: Baby pool or large plastic storage bin, water toys

1. Start by filling a baby pool or large plastic storage bin with water. A baby pool is preferred, but the large plastic storage bin will work just as well. Most likely, you'll want to do this outside.

2. Invite your child to play with a wide variety of water toys. Set a limit before they start by stating that they won't be putting their whole body in the water, just their hands and toys. This can include anything from plastic animals, to toy boats, to rubber duckies, to little people figures.

3. Allow your child to play freely, engaging in the simple play with them.

4. Follow their lead by noticing out loud what they are doing. Mimic their activities, creating a connection through the process of "parallel play."

Play Tip: This activity can be brought inside for a rainy day! Just lay down a plastic sheet and let your child play away!

"Give Your Hunger a Name"

Many children struggle with the ability to differentiate their internal sensations from their emotions (many adults do, too). Hunger is a place where this struggle frequently plays out. When kids are out of their routine or stuck inside, they can be constantly begging parents for snacks. Engage your child in this activity to help them better name the type of "hungry" they are feeling.

1. Start this activity by explaining that you will always let you child eat when they need to. (You never want to use food as a punishment or manipulation technique, because to children food is directly tied to love.)

2. Now, have your child take a deep breath, in through their nose and out through their mouth, before you (or they) interview their belly to better understand what it needs:

    a. *Belly, are you feeling hungry because you are bored?*
    b. *Belly, are you feeling hungry because you actually need a drink of water? (Sometimes our bellies feel hungry when we need a drink of water.)*
    c. *Belly, are you feeling hungry because you are sad or worried?*

3. In response to the questions, have your child draw a picture or write out their answers on the following page to help them understand their hunger.

CHAPTER SIX

Storytelling and Dramatic Play Activities

This chapter will focus on the kind of storytelling activities and pretend play many parents already engage in with their child—some of which simply enhance aspects of a child's normal daily play.

Storytelling is a powerful tool that can increase communication, strengthen connections, and create the opportunity for laughter between the parent and the child. As artist and teacher Emily Neuburger observes in her book, *Show Me a Story*, storytelling in any form can help children expand their creativity, emotional awareness, problem-solve, overcome challenges, and so much more. Joyful, playful, imaginative interactions with your child will help them feel valued—and, in turn, boost their ability to handle, interpret, and manage their emotions.

Puppet Movie

During this activity, your family will take on the task of telling a story together. Creating a story together and performing it can be harder than it sounds—it takes creative problem-solving, organization skills, and total cooperation. Working to strengthen these aspects are a useful exercise for any family. And children are happier when their family works as a team and feels united.

MATERIALS: A variety of finger and/or hand puppets or stuffed animals, video camera (or smartphone or tablet)

1. Start by explaining the rules of the story creation to your child:

   The story must be completely made up. You can't just tell a story of a book you just read or a movie you just watched. A story must have a beginning, middle, and an end. Our family must try to work together so everyone gets a role to play. When we put on the show, the puppets should do all the talking, not us.

2. As a family, decide on a theme, such as going to the movies; a party; a surprise; a big loss; fantasy; or superheroes. (Some parents might use this activity to help their child with a specific issue by picking a related theme, but no matter the theme, you and your child will benefit from this activity.)

3. Once the theme and story are created, you can write out a script for the puppets to follow. Alternatively, you can plan for total (or partial) improvisation during the performance.

4. Determine which family member is going to play each puppet. (If you don't have puppets, feel free to use stuffed animals.)

5. Once the story is ready, set up a camera to record the show (or have one family member film it).

6. Perform your story together for the camera.

7. After you finish, sit back and watch the performance together!

Play Tip: Make a big deal out of premiering your puppet movie, perhaps popping some popcorn to enjoy while you watch.

Story Song

Many parents tell me they struggle to get information from their child after a school day. "How was your day?" they may ask, only to elicit a one-word response: "Fine." The goal of this activity is to offer your child a playful way to talk about their day. By engaging your child in the creation of a song, you can entice them to share details they might not have shared otherwise.

1. It's best to start this activity in a more spontaneous way rather than explaining how it works to your child first.

2. Start the story off to a simple tune that both you and your child recognize (for example, "Twinkle, Twinkle, Little Star" or "The Farmer in the Dell.") As the parent, you will start the story off with a little bit about your day, using a prompt such as: *Once upon a time, I had a busy day, where I went to work and got stuck in traffic on the way!*

3. Pass the story off to your child, encouraging them to add another line to the song, using a stage whisper to prompt them: *Okay, it's your turn, can you sing me a line about your day?*

4. Pass the song back and forth a few times, until you and your child have shared different parts of your day.

Play Tip: This is a great game to play in the car, especially if you are working to wean your child off of screen time during car rides!

When You Were a Baby

Children love to hear stories about when they were a baby. Many children have heard some type of story already about themselves as a baby, often revolving around things like how much they cried or how little they slept. The goal of this activity is to connect with your child on all the aspects you loved about them as a baby. This type of story emphasizes to your child how special they are to you.

1. Start this activity snuggled up on the couch with your child.

2. Begin by letting them know you are going to tell them a story about when they were just a tiny baby, being sure to include specific things about how wonderful they were, and things they were able to accomplish. For example:

> Once upon a time, you were a tiny baby. You would snuggle in my arms all day. You had soft hair, big shining eyes, and you would smile at me. I loved to watch you sleep! When you would cry, I would walk around the house holding you, letting you know it was okay to cry. You loved to drink your milk and look at the doggie. You started to grow bigger and learn to crawl all around and play. You were the best baby in the world!

Play Tip: If you and your child are willing, you could play the baby game, and rock them like you used to and sing them a lullaby.

The Story of "I See You"

Many parents tell me that when their child is in a moment of panic, tantrum, or outrage, it can feel challenging to calm them down. I find this to be especially true when your child is tired, hungry, or overstimulated. During moments like these, parents may have an angry, knee-jerk reaction or dish out a punishment they later regret or don't follow through on. This activity, which I adapted from Echo Parenting & Education's concept of "Empathy Books," is effective in building an empathetic connection with your child.

1. The next time your child is having a tantrum over something simple, like letting a sibling take a turn with a toy before them, take a moment to consider a story about your child's experience. Once you have identified that your child's outburst is not a safety concern, take out this book (or any piece of paper) and start to write the story of "I see you," while narrating out loud.

2. The story of "I see you" can go something like this:

   > Once upon a time, there was a little girl named Mae, who was smart, funny, and brave. Her family loved her very, very much! One day, she asked her mom if she could have cake for breakfast and her mom said no. This made Mae feel upset. The mommy could see that Mae was very sad, upset, and didn't understand why she couldn't have cake. The end.

3. Use simple text to best help express how your child is feeling. You can add in simple pictures or drawings throughout.

Play Tip: It is extremely important to engage in this activity with a gentle, genuine tone of concern. If you find yourself too angry or agitated to use a soft tone, do not use this activity.

Story Stones

Story stones are a fun, creative way to engage your child in storytelling. The first aspect of this activity will involve creating the stones. After the story stones are created, you and your child can use them over and over again to tell tales about your worries, fears, and dreams—or simply to spark playful imagination!

MATERIALS:

Small, smooth stones

Acrylic paint

Paint markers

Permanent markers

Magazine paper

Mod podge

1. Start by washing the stones to ensure they are clean and smooth.

2. Next, think of different components of a story and create a list of different images to create on each stone, like houses, trees, flowers, sun, clouds, castles, mythical creatures, household items, bugs, people, animals, cars, boats, food—anything goes!

3. Use paint, paint markers, permanent markers, and/or magazine images attached to the stones with mod podge to create different pictures on each stone.

4. Once the stones are created, use them to tell a story, taking turns with your child and adding different details as you deploy different stones.

Play Tip: Take this game on the road! Place a few different stones in a bag and bring them with you. This is a great way to break your child away from a screen if you find them playing screen-based games too often in the car or at a restaurant.

Puppet Note Pass

This game was actually created by a client of mine during one of our sessions, early on in my career. I've often used it since, as it's a great way to engage your child in conversation about a topic they struggle to open up about. The puppets are used to help your child feel less pressure talking about themselves, because they will be speaking about their puppet's problems, not their own! In sessions, therapists tend to use this communication style to create distance between the child and their problem.

MATERIALS: Two puppets or stuffed animals, blank paper (sticky notes work well)

1. Have your child select a puppet that they want to be and a puppet for you to be. (If you do not have puppets, stuffed animals will also work.)

2. During this game, you and your child will not be communicating verbally. You will be passing messages back and forth between the puppets.

3. Start by writing a message to your child from your puppet, making sure to direct the message to your child's puppet, not them: *Hello Mr. Raccoon, how do you feel today?*

4. Pass the message to their puppet, instructing them to write you a message back.

5. Engage in conversation back and forth, allowing the puppets to "talk" to each other about whatever they would like to speak about, through the note passing. You could ask your child how they felt about a recent challenging situation, or an upcoming event at school.

Play Tip: If your child struggles with writing, use simple pictures to communicate instead—basic stick figures, feelings, faces, and a few words would do the trick!

Photo Book Story

Most children love to see pictures of themselves from when they were a baby. This activity facilitates storytelling about your child's early years, using pictures to help enhance the experience. It's a great way for you to connect with your child, allowing you to both rejoice in the relationship you've cultivated. In particular, having your child hear you talk about that time in a positive and loving way helps solidify the narrative that they are loved and important.

MATERIALS: Family photos of you and your child

1. Allow your child to look through photos of themselves from when they were a baby.

2. Stop them at the photo of your choice and tell them a story about that moment.

3. Try to share as much detail as possible, including sensory information, such as what you saw them doing, how it made you feel, or even what it smelled like in the moment!

4. Repeat for as many photos as you and your child like.

Play Tip: Create a photo storybook together. Allow your child to choose pictures of themselves from childhood and paste them into a book or journal, writing the story of each moment to go along with it!

Doctor Play

Many children will spontaneously gravitate toward play that helps them overcome challenges. Offering specific opportunities for your child to engage in theme-based play will increase their ability to share their worries and develop their ability to overcome them. Many parents have seen the fear in their child's eyes right before they get another round of shots or heard the terrified screams when the doctor simply wants to listen to the child's heartbeat with the stethoscope. Allowing your child to play about these fears and worries will help them manage stress related to visiting the doctor's office.

MATERIALS: Toy doctor's kit (optional), dress-up doctor clothes (optional—white lab coat, face mask, etc.), stuffed animals, dolls

1. Invite your child to play doctor, use the toy doctor's kit and dress-up clothes to make them feel powerful in the role. (If you do not have a kit or dress-up clothes, use what you have around the house and encourage your child to use their imagination!)

2. Allow them to perform medical procedures on you, stuffed animals, and/or dolls, like shots, checking heart rate, listening to breathing, and so on.

3. Intently engage with them in this play, noticing out loud what stuffed animals might feel or what they might be thinking during the medical procedure. For example:

   a. *Oh, I wonder if the little turtle is nervous before he gets his shot*
   b. *I wonder what would make the little turtle feel better?*

Play Tip: Even if your child struggles with going to the doctor, allow this type of play to be just that–play! Despite the subject matter, it should still feel joyful and lighthearted.

Viewpoint Story

A healthy part of any child's development is their ability to see things from someone else's point of view. When we can understand what an experience is like for someone else, we increase our ability to empathize and connect with others. During this activity, you'll have them listen to and understand your viewpoint of a moment in time.

MATERIALS: Markers, crayons, colored pencils

1. First, choose a moment in time when your child accomplished something. Let your child know you are going to create a story together about that moment.

2. Explain that you are going to be the author of the story, meaning you write the words; your child will be the illustrator, meaning they draw the pictures.

3. Narrate the story out loud as you write, making sure to emphasize what you were thinking at the time. This helps your child learn to see an experience they had from another person's point of view. For example:

   One day, you were learning to ride a bike. At first, I was feeling a bit nervous when you decided to try to pedal without any training wheels. I was thinking to myself: *You can do it.* I saw you push on the pedals and pause. I wondered if you were thinking: *This is scary.* You looked at me, smiled, and biked away. I saw just how brave and strong you are!

4. After you write the words about your child's accomplishment, ask them to draw pictures that describe what it was like for them in the space provided on the following page.

Play Tip: This type of joint viewpoint activity will help your child understand how your experience could be different or similar to their own. After you create the story, talk about what you notice the similarities or differences were.

Magic Potion

The goal of this activity is to help your child overcome a challenge by using magical thinking. Magical thinking is a powerful and creative part of childhood. This aspect of a child's mind allows them to believe in superheroes, fairy tales, and Santa. When a child can use this as a skill, they are able to overcome a worry, fear, or challenge. This activity asks your child to use their "magical" powers to feel braver and stronger! This is a creative, silly way to help your child connect with this joyful part of childhood.

1. Start by identifying something your child is struggling to overcome, like sleeping in their own bed, trying a new sport, or doing their homework.

2. Tell your child that you want them to know a secret—that they have the magic inside of them to overcome this big challenge.

3. Explain that, in order to help their magic powers become stronger, you are going to make a magic potion filled with all the things they need to be able to overcome this challenge.

4. Use the following page to write out all the things they need to overcome the challenge. They should be figurative things, not literal things, like calm, Superman strength, or Wonder Woman confidence. Get creative!

5. After they pretend to take the potion, encourage your child to draw a picture of themselves overcoming this challenge in the space provided.

Play Tip: For more elaborate play, make a liquid magic potion. Fill a cup with water and add in food coloring. Have your child imagine themselves overcoming the challenge as they create the potion!

Magic Mailbox

This activity is intended to inspire your child's imagination, playfulness, and magical thinking, which can help them solve problems, overcome worries, and gain confidence. You'll help them create a magic mailbox that allows them to communicate with their toys, stuffed animals, or imaginary friends.

MATERIALS:

Box, jar, or other container   Beads   Glue

Stickers   Sequins   Paper

Markers

1. Start by helping your child create a magical mailbox. This mailbox will be used to send messages back and forth between them and an imaginary friend or toy.

2. Create the magic box using some type of container, encouraging your child to decorate the mailbox with stickers, markers, beads, and sequins—all of which will emphasize its "magical" properties.

3. Playing pretend, choose a toy figure, stuffed animal, doll, or imaginary friend that your child will send stories to and from via the magical mailbox.

4. Have your child write a message to the toy of their choice. They could ask about the toy's worries, fears, likes, or dislikes. Encourage your child to be playful and creative—any type of question goes.

5. When your child is not around, write them a message back, making it appear to come from that toy.

Play Tip: Use the magic mailbox to leave tiny treasures and/or gifts from their special friends as well!

Story Chain

During this activity, you and your child will write a page of story at a time over the course of a week or a month. It will prove a beneficial challenge for a child who struggles with self-control, as you are only able to write one page of the story a day. Each day, you will create a new page of the story together, to help them boost their creativity and ability to handle delayed gratification.

MATERIALS: Index cards, drawing materials (crayons, markers, paints, and/or colored pencils)

1. Start by explaining to your child that you're going to create a story together.

2. Explain to your child that what's different about this story is that it will take a very long time to tell.

3. Brainstorm with your child who the main character should be. It could be a real person, an imaginary person, an animal, or even a character similar to your own child.

4. If you and your child are struggling to start the story, choose a story you both already love to read and create what would happen in the sequel to the story.

5. Start by writing the first page of the story on an index card. Allow your child to draw a picture for each page and do the writing if they are willing and able.

6. Add to the story the next day, adding a page to the story each day for at least a week.

7. Once the story is complete, put the index cards together to make a book!

Play Tip: Hang each index card on the wall in a place in your house that everyone can see. Make a big, long index card chain along the wall as you create the story!

CHAPTER SEVEN

Challenge Activities

Challenge is a part of daily life, no matter your age. But when we're able to exhibit confidence in the face of an obstacle, we strengthen our self-esteem, problem-solving skills, and impulse control, often because it takes control and patience to learn something new. Playing challenging games, like the ones included in this chapter, is a powerful way for your child to learn these skills; according to the paper "The Neurobiological Power of Play," when children learn these skills during a playful, joyful moment, their brains store them more effectively. Consequently, they'll be able to more readily access them during challenging moments in the future.

Some of these games create opportunities where your child might lose. Losing a game can be a big challenge for many kids, and learning how to handle losing well is a useful skill. Other games in this chapter have no clear winner, just a playful competitive nature that allows your child to focus on the skills without the added pressure of performance.

Red Light, Green Light

This classic game doesn't require much introduction. Although you've likely played it before, you may not be aware of the amazing benefits of such a simple game. Red Light, Green Light challenges your child to follow verbal directions, as well as exercise impulse control. Many play therapists use this game in session to help children practice these vital skills.

MATERIALS: Red "stop" sign (optional), Green "go" sign (optional), Yellow "slow motion" sign (optional)

1. Determine who is going to be the stoplight first. This person will be telling the "cars"—or, the other person—what to do by flashing the signs (if using). Feel free to use household objects or clothes with corresponding colors as signs.

2. Use whatever space you have available to play this game: your living room, your backyard, or your child's bedroom.

3. If you are a "car," you must follow these rules:

    a. *Green light means GO*
    b. *Red light means STOP*
    c. *Yellow light means slow motion with deep breaths*

4. Take turns being both the car and the stoplight.

Play Tip: Don't forget to be a good challenge coach! Any time your child is showing signs that they are able to follow the rules of the game, notice that out loud with extra enthusiasm: "Oh wow, you know just when to slow down and when to stop!"

Bubble Tag

I use bubbles frequently with clients to help with relaxation and calming, often in conjunction with deep breaths to close out a session. It was during one of these moments that one of my clients and I found ourselves engaged in a playful game of bubble tag. This is a game that appears to be a challenge but is really a powerful, playful way to get your child to take deep, full breaths. And when we take deep, full breaths, we send the message to our bodies that we are safe.

MATERIALS: Bubble wands and bubble solution

1. Start by explaining the rules of the game to your child: *Every player will have their own container of bubbles. The goal of the game is to try to "tag" the other player with the bubbles that you blow!*

2. Before you begin, make sure you and your child's bubble wands are filled with bubble solution.

3. Next, take a breath in through your nose and breathe out through your mouth, making as many bubbles as you can.

4. Explain to your child that, the bigger bubbles they blow, the more likely they are to tag their partner.

5. Run around and dodge to try to escape getting tagged by the bubbles!

Play Tip: For safety purposes, before the game starts, establish that bubbles are not for blowing in each other's face or eyes. This will help reduce your need for correction in the midst of this joyful connection.

Walk, Stop, Sit

The goal of this activity is to increase your child's self-control and ability to follow verbal directions. I learned this activity at a Little Flower children's yoga training and continue to be blown away by how engaging and challenging it is—even for adults! I have since incorporated this into many play therapy sessions and find children are able to benefit from the playful challenges that this game offers.

1. Start by explaining the rules of the game to your child:

   > This is a challenging listening game. You are going to be doing the opposite of what I say. For example, when I say 'walk,' you are going to stop, and when I say 'stop,' you are going to walk! It is going to be a really big challenge!

2. The opposite actions are as follows (though feel free to get creative with you child and make up your own!):

   a. WALK means STOP
   b. STOP means WALK
   c. SIT means STAND
   d. STAND means SIT
   e. DANCE mean FREEZE
   f. FREEZE means DANCE

3. Once the rules are explained, start the game by calling out the action you want them to do the opposite of.

4. Take turns being the person who calls the action and the person who has to do the opposite.

Play Tip: For an added level of playfulness, engage in the opposite action with your child instead of just watching them do it. Join in on the fun!

Giant Gameboard

Turn your living room or your child's playroom into a life-size gameboard! The goal of this activity is to incorporate all the challenging aspects of a board game into a full-body experience! Creating opportunities for your child to engage in large muscle movement and creativity can help them manage their emotions and behavior. This game is perfect for the entire family—particularly when you're stuck inside on a rainy day!

MATERIALS: Paper, drawing materials (crayons, markers, paints, and/or colored pencils), dice, timer, play money (optional)

1. Start by engaging your child in the task of creating a game. Use simple rules and allow for creativity. Example rules may include:

    a. *Roll the dice to know how many spaces to move.*
    b. *Each space will have a silly task on it, such as: jump on one foot, take a deep breath, find something in another room, and so on. If you can complete the task before time runs out, you earn a point or play money.*

2. Use paper to create the spaces around the room. You and your child will be the game pieces, moving around the room every time you roll!

Play Tip: Anything goes for this game—allow your child to be as creative as possible!

Imagination Game

Allow your child to create and develop the game of their dreams. The only rule is this: once the game starts, you cannot, under any circumstances, change the rules! Empowering your child to create the game increases their interest, but challenging them to adhere to their own rules can help boost their emotional tolerance and flexibility. I often play this game in session with kids ages eight to ten, who are really into games but hate the idea of losing.

MATERIALS: Dice, play chips, chess pawns, checkers, marbles, Monopoly money and/or other miscellaneous game pieces, crayons and/or markers

1. Allow your child to create the game they want to create, using the sample gameboard on the following page to help you design it. The game can have any purpose, goal, or method, and can use the miscellaneous game pieces in any way they like!

2. Use the designated space on the following page to list the rules for the game. These must be followed once the game starts!

Play Tip: Do your best to vocalize your own emotions during the game, talking out loud about how it is hard to lose, even if you still really enjoy playing: *Aww, I lost a turn. It makes me mad to lose a turn, but I know I'll get another chance soon!*

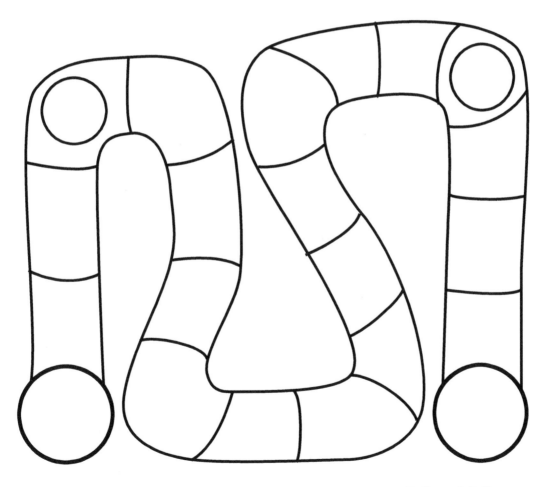

"Can You Build It?"

This activity, perfect for the curious child, works to build your child's creative problem-solving skills. Learning to solve problems while we play strengthens the brain's ability to access those solutions in the future.

MATERIALS: Plastic straws, toothpicks, index cards, paper clips, glue

1. Explain to your child that you are going to try to build the biggest, strongest tower possible.

2. Using only the materials listed above, try to build and create a tower.

3. Work together with your child to let them explore and problem-solve during this challenging activity, doing your best to not solve the problem for them.

Play Tip: Increase the challenge by adding a timer and a limited amount of time to build the tower.

Bubblegum Chew

This game's simplicity belies its many powerful uses. It allows your child to engage their nervous system in the grounding efforts of deep pressure and sensory input, as well as in the soothing aspects of deep breathing. In addition, blowing big bubbles with gum provides an added challenge to keep your child engaged and excited.

MATERIALS: Double Bubble bubble gum (or another tough-to-chew bubble gum)

1. Offer your child a piece of bubble gum—the harder the gum is to chew at first, the better!

2. Show your child how to take a deep bubble breath by breathing in through the nose and blowing the air out through your mouth to make a bubble.

3. Make it a playful competition by trying to blow bigger bubbles than each other!

Play Tip: After a full day of learning and focusing at school, many parents tell me their children often experience tantrums when they return home. This game has all the aspects needed to help regulate your child's nervous system following a long day.

Animal Tag

This is a great game to play to release some excess energy. It's a classic game of tag mixed with a level of playful imagination. It's best to play with more than two people, so get the whole family involved if you can! The powerful combination of movement, playfulness, and joy all help to build your child's imagination and self-esteem.

1. Use your imagination to decide what type of animal habitat you want to be in, such as the ocean, jungle, farm, or desert.

2. One person will pretend to be the bigger stronger animal (e.g., a shark or lion).

3. The strong, powerful animal will be the hunter and try to tag all the other animals.

4. Take turns being the hunter and remember to keep this game light and playful.

Play tip: Don't forget your animal sounds! This game will stay silly and playful if you fully take on the role of your animal.

Spitball Target

This playful challenge activity works to engage your child's senses and competitive nature. During this game, you will be blowing spitballs at a target, trying to earn the most points! For success, it requires focus, attention, deep breaths, and sportsmanship, which are skills every child should practice.

MATERIALS: Paper, markers, tape, toilet paper, plastic straws

1. Start by creating a target for the game: Draw one large circle, filling it in with smaller circles leading to a bullseye, similar to a dart board. Add a different point value for each circle.

2. Hang the target on the wall with a piece of tape.

3. Set an important limit before you explain the rules: *Spitballs are not to be used or made any other time than during this game! Not in school, at a restaurant, or when you want to bug your sibling. ONLY during this time!*

4. Explain the rules of the game to your child:

    a. *First, we will roll pieces of toilet paper into small little balls.*
    b. *Next, chew the paper a bit to make the perfect spitball.*
    c. *Place the spitball at the end of the straw.*
    d. *The goal of the game is to blow spitballs at the target, earning as many points as possible.*
    e. *Hit the bullseye three times and earn the most points to win the game!*

5. Take turns making spitballs and blowing them at the target until there is a winner.

Play Tip: Problem-solve what size spitball works the best! This game is a bit messy, and for some, a bit gross, but your child will be blown away by your willingness to play something so silly.

Cotton Ball Pass

At first glance, this activity that I adapted from Theraplay (see page 24) seems incredibly easy, but it can be quite difficult for young children. The game requires breath control, eye contact, and making deliberate, tactical movements. The more chances you can give your child to experience the joy of mastering simple yet challenging tasks, the more confident and self-assured they will become.

MATERIALS: Cotton balls

1. Sit facing your child. This is best done with both of you sitting on the floor, cross-legged, with your knees touching.

2. Start by placing a cotton ball in your hand, and explain the rules of the game: *The goal of the game is to try to pass this cotton ball back and forth between us, using only our breath.*

3. Cup your hands to cradle the cotton ball, gently blowing it into your child's cupped hands.

4. Pass the cotton ball back and forth as many times as possible without letting it blow out of your hands!

Play Tip: Try to do this without any words! Come up with a silly face to make to let your child know you are ready to pass them the cotton ball.

Freeze Dance

This is a classic game that many children have played before. In it, you are asking your child to freeze right in the middle of doing something they probably like to do: dance! Learning to stop doing something they like, even when they don't want to, is an important skill for every child to learn.

MATERIALS: Music and speakers

1. Start by explaining the rules of the game to your child: *We'll dance along to the music until it stops, at which point, we have to FREEZE! When the music starts up again, we'll continue dancing.*

2. Decide who is going to be the DJ; this person could be a parent, a sibling, or another child.

3. Decide who is going to be the dancer—the more, the merrier!

4. The DJ will start the music and decide when it is time to FREEZE. Play the music for as long as you like and have the dancers freeze as often as you like!

5. Take turns being both the DJ and the dancer.

Play Tip: Challenge your child to freeze in the pose of their favorite superhero, and don't forget to join in the fun!

Obstacle Course Challenge

When you and your child work through a challenge that's both physical and mental, as this one is, you help them build the confidence, problem-solving skills, and cognitive flexibility they need to succeed in school and beyond. This activity is perfect for when you're stuck inside on a rainy day.

MATERIALS: Scissors, construction paper, painter's tape

1. First, find a room in your house that has a decent amount of open-floor space.

2. Cut out large shapes from the construction paper (see step 4). Lay them out in any pattern you like and tape them to the floor. The idea here is to use them to create some type of path across the open space.

3. Once the course is complete, explain the rules of the course to your child: *You need to try to make it from one side of the course to another; as you step on each new shape, you must complete the movement task to be able to move to the next shape.*

4. Assign a movement task to each shape, such as:

    a. Zig-zag: Walk heel-to-toe
    b. Circle: 10 jumping jacks
    c. Triangle: 10 squats
    d. Square: Take 5 deep breaths
    e. Diamond: 10 push-ups
    f. Handprints or Footprints: For a fun extra challenge, try to walk along this path, keeping your hands and feet on the paper prints at all times! Use a timer for an added level of challenge. See how quickly your child can complete the course, working to improve each time!

Play Tip: Have your child bring their favorite toy along. They can run matchbox cars along the course or have their favorite stuffed animal try to complete the task!

Marble Run

For this activity, you and your child will be using household materials to create a racetrack for a marble. The kind of playful creativity and problem-solving required here will increase your child's ability to think analytically in the midst of a challenge. This activity is particularly well-suited to the aspiring engineer who might need a bit more patience.

MATERIALS:

Empty toilet paper or paper towel rolls

Painter's tape

Scissors

Marble

Basket or cup

1. Start by explaining to your child that you are going to use the materials you've collected to build a marble racetrack.

2. Find a wall that is free to use in your home.

3. Chart the racetrack by placing the empty rolls against the wall. Have your child use their imagination and creativity to build a racetrack of any size or shape.

4. Using the painter's tape, help your child attach the marble racetrack to the wall.

5. Place a basket or cup on the floor at the end of the track and let your marble run the course!

Play Tip: Make more than one course! If you have more than one child, allow them to each create their own and race each other!

CHAPTER EIGHT

Outdoor Activities

Today's children live more structured lives than children of prior generations, attending school for almost eight hours a day before participating in one or multiple afterschool activities and an hour or so of homework. This degree of structure can be a positive thing, but there are downsides as well—namely, that children are spending less and less time outdoors. Meanwhile, a growing body of research, summarized in the book, *Nature Play at Home*, shows that spending time outdoors has positive effects on an individual's overall health, sleep patterns, and mood, even decreasing symptoms of ADHD, anxiety, and depression.

As outdoor play continues to disappear from our children's lives, helping to increase your child's engagement in the kinds of activities featured here only stands to benefit your child. Nothing can truly beat the power of totally unstructured outdoor play, but these activities will help give you and your child a jumping-off point for outdoor creativity and connection.

Choose Your Own Adventure

When children have a screen constantly giving them prompts, making noise, and feeding their need for stimulation, it can be extremely hard to access the creativity sparked from the comparably quiet aspects of unstructured play. Help your child engage in this vital type of play by framing the following activity as an "adventure."

MATERIALS: An explorer figure, such as an animal figure, baby doll, stuffed animal, or superhero figure

1. Start by explaining to your child that you are going to allow them to create their own outdoor adventure today.

2. Have them choose one or two toys to bring along on the adventure. Choose a toy that is sturdy enough to handle the outdoors. (I would advise against using your child's favorite sleep-time stuffed animal, as it may get dirty.)

3. Find an outdoor space that allows for you and your child to safely play. This could be a local park, wooded area, or your own backyard.

4. Explain that you are going to take their toy on any type of adventure they want through the outdoors. Anything goes!

5. The only rule is that they have to help keep the toy safe. Offer other safety rules depending on your comfort level with the play space. For example, staying within eyesight or away from bodies of water without supervision.

6. Allow your child to take the lead, not offering much direction.

Play Tip: If your child is old enough for independent, outdoor play, allow for space during this activity. Be nearby if needed but allow them to use the imagination sparked during unstructured outdoor play!

I Spy a Challenge

Many of us can walk down the same street hundreds of times without noticing its simple, yet idiosyncratic details. This playful game puts a spin on the classic game of I Spy, in order to really help your child connect with the world around them and be present in their environment.

1. Start by explaining the rules of this version of I Spy to your child:

   a. *First, we will pick a color or shape we are trying to find around us.*
   b. *The goal is to find more things that are the chosen color or shape than the other person.*
   c. *The first person to find five things that are this color or shape wins!*

2. Once the rules are explained, have your child decide on a color or shape they want to search for. This game is great to play at the playground or on a walk around your neighborhood.

3. Have your child call out and point to the relevant items they see.

Play Tip: For an added challenge and level of playfulness, add in the rule of "firsts." If you are the first to see a common item that is the color your child chose, you get the point and your child cannot point out that item going forward. For example: if the chosen color is "green" and you notice a green tree first, your child cannot point to every green tree they see.

Sensational Walk

Taking a walk as a family is a great way to spend time outside. Adding in this playful element can increase your child's engagement and connection to the outdoors, as well as their awareness of their five senses.

1. Invite your child and other family members to take a walk outside. This is great to do after work and school, before your child starts their homework.

2. While on the walk, playfully engage with your child in noticing their senses on the walk. Start by having them notice their sense of sight, by prompting them to name five things they see.

3. Next, have your child notice their sense of smell by having them smell various things around them. Stop to smell different items, such as plants and flowers.

4. Engage your child's sense of touch by bringing to their attention how their feet feel in their shoes as they move across various terrains, such as the grass and the sidewalk.

5. Lastly, have your child notice their sense of hearing: What different noises can they hear around them? Do they hear birds, the wind, or cars passing by?

6. Have your child notice how the things they've sensed have changed as they walk.

7. After you return from your walk, have your child complete the activities on the following page (if using) to help document what they noticed on the walk.

Play Tip: Notice aloud what your own senses are picking up to help your child connect with their own senses.

Draw a picture of something you saw

Draw a picture of something you felt

Draw a picture of something you smelled

Draw a picture of something you heard

Outdoor Kitchen

Children love to play-act what's going on around them. For many children, that means domestic play, such as "kitchen" and "house." When you mix that natural drive with the elements of the outdoors, your child will discover endless hours of fun!

MATERIALS: Kitchen items (pots, pans, cups, cupcake tins, ladles, scoops, and/or other utensils), watering can, basin

1. Start by building the outdoor mud kitchen play space. First, dedicate an area to be the kitchen. You could use an old table, bench, or even large, round logs. Use what you have available to create a somewhat contained space.

2. Stock the play space with any type of kitchen items available. Search thrift stores and your child's toys to find items you can get dirty.

3. Next, find (or make) the mud. Mix soil of any kind with water in a basin to make the perfect ingredient for mixing, making recipes, and creating fun concoctions.

4. Fill another container with just enough water to allow your child to make more mud if they wish.

5. Allow your child to play with the mud and toys in any way they like! Creativity and freedom are paramount during this type of play.

Play Tip: Don't be afraid to get messy with your child! Playing in the mud is a magical marker of childhood.

Tandem Swings

The goal of this swinging activity is to combine the powerful aspects of the outdoors with beneficial nervous system activation. According to Doreit Bialer and Dr. Lucy Jane Miller's book, *No Longer a Secret*, swinging actually stimulates your vestibular system—a part of our sensory system that plays a role in emotion management. The more activation this part of our nervous system gets, the better we can regulate our emotions. Swinging next to your child, and trying to move in tandem, creates a sense of connection in the midst of this grounding activity.

1. Find a set of swings. For this activity, you need two swings that are next to each other.

2. Sit next to your child and work to get swinging at the same pace.

3. Add in this playful song to increase the connection (to the tune of "The More We Get Together"):

   The more we swing together
   Together, together
   The more we swing together
   The happier we'll be

Play Tip: For an added sense of playfulness, try to swing in tandem at different speeds: slow-motion, medium, and fast.

Affirmation Hopscotch

This classic game needs no introduction. But with a slight twist, you'll combine the playful movement of hopscotch with the power of positive self-talk. Play can create connections in the brain to emphasize the meaningful aspects of this kind of talk.

MATERIALS: Sidewalk chalk, beanbag or small stone

1. Using the sidewalk chalk, draw out a simple hopscotch design on your driveway or sidewalk. As a reminder, a hopscotch design is created by stacking a pattern of squares to create a path. The rows will alternate in width: the first row will have one box, the second will have two, the third will have one, and so on.

2. Instead of writing numbers in each box, write a different positive affirmation. These may include the following:

   a. *I am strong.*
   b. *I am brave.*
   c. *I can handle it.*
   d. *I am smart.*

3. Stand behind the first block and take turns tossing a beanbag or small stone, trying to land it on one of the squares.

4. If it is your turn, say the positive statement the beanbag or stone lands on as you try to hop along to the pattern, only hopping as far as the beanbag or stone goes.

5. Take turns tossing the beanbag or stone onto the hopscotch board, saying the positive statements along the way!

Play Tip: As you write out the positive statements, talk about different times you and your child felt that way about yourselves.

Wishing Garden

The goal of this activity is to create a special place outdoors for you and your child to bring your worries and fill them with wishes. Creating a specific location for these concerns can help your child unburden themselves of anxious feelings.

MATERIALS: Stones, non-toxic washable paint, flowers

1. Choose a section of your yard or garden (or even a window box or secluded area of a nearby park) that can be dedicated to your "wishing garden." Use stones to create the borders of this small section.

2. Help your child to paint and decorate the "magic wishing stones." Once they're done, have your child stack their wishing stones in the wishing garden.

3. Once your wishing garden is complete, have your child sit near the garden with a worry in mind.

4. Instruct them to take a deep breath through their nose, using their exhale to expel their worry and trap it in the wishing stones.

5. If possible, plant flowers together in the wishing garden!

Play Tip: If you notice your child is worried or overwhelmed, take them to the wishing garden and have them breathe their worries into the garden.

Land Art

The goal of this activity is to help your child explore the natural environment around them. They will be collecting items they find and using them to create an art piece. This creative, art-based exercise is a great way to get your child to forge a connection to nature, especially if they struggle with unstructured outdoor play.

1. Choose a place to explore with your child. It can be anywhere from your backyard, to the park, to the beach.

2. Take your child on an outdoor adventure to this place to collect things in nature that can be used to create a work of art, such as leaves, sticks, stones, rocks, pine cones, shells, pebbles, and the like.

3. Choose a place to make your art. This could be on the grass, sand, or a picnic table.

4. Talk about what to create using the items you've collected. For example, they could make a face or a sunset scene or even a picture of your family. Let your child's imagination run wild!

5. Follow your child's lead, allowing them to spark their imagination and creativity.

Play Tip: Take a picture of your child's creation so they can remember their piece of art!

Imagine That!

The goal of this activity is to let your child explore their creativity, imagination, and observation skills. All of these things build coping skills and cognitive flexibility that can help them with their schoolwork and regulating their emotions.

MATERIALS: Drawing materials (crayons, markers, paint, and/or colored pencils)

1. Pick a place outside that you and your child enjoy. This could be a park or your backyard.

2. First, have your child draw what they see around them.

3. Next, have them add to their drawing three things they wish were there. For example: dragons, gold, or a mountain of candy.

Play Tip: If you are doing this activity in your own yard, hang a big piece of paper on a fence or use sidewalk chalk instead, letting your child create a large scene in the driveway or on the sidewalk!

Cloud Watching

This is an age-old outdoor activity, enjoyed by children and adults alike. The goal is simple: to help your child slow down, be present, and use their imagination. The more your child is able to practice these skills, the more emotionally well-balanced they will become.

MATERIALS: Blanket, crayons, markers

1. Spread a blanket on the ground to make a cozy place for you and your child to lay down.

2. Snuggle with your child on the blanket, looking up together at the sky.

3. Use your imagination to see what shapes, images, and pictures can be created out of the clouds.

4. Help your child draw the cloud shapes they see on the following page. Given the lack of external stimuli, this will help keep their focus on an activity—especially if your child is used to using a tablet or handheld video game console for entertainment.

Play Tip: Bring a snack and enjoy a picnic while watching the clouds go by.

Feelings Scavenger Hunt

We can often miss small, beautiful things around us. This activity will help your child slow down and connect with themselves and the world around them.

MATERIALS: Magnifying glass (optional), binoculars (optional)

1. Start by choosing a place to take your feelings scavenger hunt. This type of activity is great to play on a hiking path or in a wooded area.

2. Explain to your child that you are going to search for things in their environment that make them feel different types of feelings. Examples may include: butterflies, trees, a ravine, spiders, sunshine, wind, and so on.

3. After they find these things in their environment, they will study them and draw a picture of them on the following page to better understand why these different things in nature make them feel different ways. Use the binoculars and magnifying glass (if using) to look at things far away or close up. For example:

   a. *A big cliff could make someone feel nervous.*
   b. *Seeing the sunshine could make someone feel happy.*
   c. *Seeing a squirrel could make someone laugh.*

Play Tip: Collect some of the things that your child finds (if they are portable), such as leaves, rocks, and the like. Save them for future exploration!

Find and draw a picture of one thing that makes you feel happy

Find and draw a picture of one thing that makes your feel nervous

Find and draw a picture of one thing that makes you feel scared

Find and draw a picture of one thing that makes you laugh

Find and draw a picture of one thing that makes you feel mad

Find and draw a picture of one thing that makes you feel sad

CHAPTER NINE

Relaxation and Breathing

Breathwork is a valuable tool any individual can use. Our breath is so powerful, it can shift our internal state in a matter of minutes. When we learn to purposefully use our breath, we are able to exert greater control over our emotions. Every parent wants their child to be able to press pause, breathe, and calm themself down. Learning how to create space in the moment before we react to a stressful person or situation is a crucial skill—not just for children, but for adults, too.

Bubble Breaths

The goal of this activity is to help your child learn how to take a deep, full breath. Not all breaths create the same response in the body. When we learn to exhale longer than we inhale, we send the message to our bodies and brains that we are safe.

MATERIALS: Bubble wand and bubble solution

1. Follow these steps with your child to help them learn how to take a full, soothing breath.

2. First, dip your bubble wand into the bubble solution.

3. Inhale through your nose.

4. Try to exhale longer than your inhale by blowing your air out through your mouth toward the bubble wand. The goal is to exhale longer than you inhale. The number of bubbles you blow doesn't matter, nor does the size of the bubbles you blow. This is simply the best way to teach your child how to actually take a soothing, deep breath.

5. Have your child repeat steps two through four as many times as they'd like.

Play Tip: After each bubble breath, encourage your child to try to pop the bubbles as fast as they can!

Giant Bubble

Teaching children to take deep, full breaths in the midst of a challenge will help them learn to breathe when they need it most. Working to blow a giant bubble takes focus, breath control, and patience.

MATERIALS: Bubble wand and bubble solution

1. Start by dipping your bubble wand into the bubbles.
2. Next, take a deep breath in through your nose.
3. Exhale at medium speed, with your lips in the shape of a circle.
4. This combination will help you blow a giant bubble!
5. Try to blow as many giant bubbles as you can.

Play Tip: Normalize how hard this is by talking out loud about the challenge. You could say something like, *Wow, this takes hard work and focus. I tried all the right things and still didn't get it!*

Bubble Freeze

The goal of this activity is to help your child learn how to both take a deep, full breath and to work at controlling their impulses. Impulse control is a common area of weakness for many children. Doing this in a playful, soothing way will increase your child's ability to master the task.

MATERIALS: Bubble wand and bubble solution

1. Explain to your child that you are going to be playing a "freeze" game. Follow these steps along with them.

2. First, dip your bubble wand into the bubble solution.

3. Inhale through your nose.

4. Try to exhale longer than you inhale as you blow the air out through your mouth toward the bubble wand.

5. After you blow out all of your air, freeze!

6. Stay frozen until all the bubbles pop around you.

Play Tip: Help your child notice what it feels like in their body to be completely frozen with questions like, *How does it feel in your body when we stand still?* and *Was it hard to stand still and not pop the bubbles?*

Superhero Breath

The goal of this activity is to pair deep breathing with the strong characteristics of your child's favorite superhero. Because play increases our ability to learn a skill, this activity will help your child access deep breathing in times of distress.

MATERIALS: Superhero cape (optional)

1. With your child, identify their favorite superhero.

2. Ask your child to show you how that superhero would stand if they were feeling really strong and brave (helping them put on the cape, if applicable). Copy this superhero pose with your body as well.

3. Now, encourage your child to take a deep breath, in through the nose and out through the mouth, as they stand strong like their favorite superhero.

Play Tip: Have your child imagine a challenging or difficult moment when they would need to channel their favorite superhero and their powerful breathing tools. Have them pretend to be in that moment and overcome it with their superhero powers and breath!

Hard Spaghetti

Progressive muscle relaxation is the act of tightening and relaxing different muscles in your body to create a soothing experience for the nervous system—it's great to do before bed or as you are helping your child calm down. I learned this particular activity, which incorporates progressive muscle relaxation, during graduate school, and have used it in sessions ever since!

1. Ask your child if they know what spaghetti looks like *before* it is cooked. If they don't know, explain to your child that before spaghetti is cooked it is hard and stiff; demonstrate with your body by putting your feet together and arms straight at your side, with all your muscles tightened.

2. Ask your child how spaghetti looks *after* it has been cooked. Explain to your child that it is wiggly; demonstrate with your body by getting loose and wiggly.

3. Now, show them how to do the full "hard spaghetti" breath:

    a. *As you take a deep breath in, make your body hard like a spaghetti noodle.*
    b. *On your exhale make, your body loose and wiggly like a cooked noodle.*

Play Tip: Challenge your child by trying to make your body look like their favorite noodle: *Can you make your body look like a spiral noodle, elbow noodle, or even a meatball?*

Back-to-Back Breathing

I learned this breathwork technique during a child's yoga training by Little Flower, an organization that provides training on yoga and mindfulness for kids. Parents are always looking for ways to get their children to slow down, breathe, and sit calmly. This is a great way to practice these skills.

1. Start by sitting back-to-back with your child.

2. Notice if your breath is moving at the same pace or a different pace than theirs.

3. Next, try to match your breathing with your child's breathing, then work to slow both your breathing down.

4. Close your eyes and have your child close theirs. Have them notice what it feels like to breathe in sync with each other.

Play Tip: Have both you and your child place one hand on your belly and one hand on your heart–see if you can feel the air going into your belly and your heart rate changing.

Elephant Breath

The goal of this type of breath is to playfully activate and energize your body. This breath is great for when you are trying to get your pokey child moving in the morning or to hype them up before something challenging.

1. Engage your child in the elephant breath by first pretending that your arm is the elephant's trunk.

2. Inhale as you bring your elephant trunk in the air, raising it above your head, looking up to the sky.

3. On the exhale, bend forward, moving your trunk toward the ground. Flutter your lips, just like an elephant spraying water from their trunk.

4. Repeat steps 2 and 3 three more times for the most energizing effect!

Play Tip: Add an element of play by trying your best to make elephant noises in-between inhales.

Lion Breath

Everyone knows that the lion is the king of the jungle. This type of breath helps your child channel the powerful nature of a lion in a soothing and grounded way.

1. Start by talking about how strong, brave, and observant lions are with your child. For example:

    a. *Did you know lions are known as the top of the animal food chain—that they are strong, brave, and confident?*
    b. *How strong do you think a lion is?*
    c. *How brave do you think they have to be to scare away things that could hurt them?*

2. Explain that this type of breath will help you both feel strong, calm, and brave.

3. Show your child how to stand or sit strong, just like a lion.

4. Inhale through your nose.

5. On the exhale, open your mouth, sticking your tongue out and forcing the air out quickly, making a "ha" sound.

6. Repeat this breath two to four times with your child.

Play Tip: Add in a playful element by practicing your strongest lion roar in between breaths.

Fairy Breath

This breath was created by one of my clients in a session. We were playfully practicing deep breathing when she instructed me on how to take a fairy breath. I have loved it ever since, and found that young children who love magic, fairies, princesses, and the like connect with this type of deep breath.

MATERIALS: Fairy wings (optional)

1. Engage your child in talking about what type of fairy they want to be:

    a. *What type of magical powers would you have?*
    b. *Where would you fly with your fairy wings?*
    c. *What color fairy dress would you be wearing?*
    d. *Are you a magic fairy, fairy princess, or both?*

2. Explain to your child that they are going to learn to breathe like a magic fairy. Follow these steps along with them.

3. Start by standing tall with your arms at your side.

4. On your inhale, raise your arms up along your side, as if you were flapping your fairy wings.

5. On the exhale, flap your wings up and down.

6. Repeat as many times as your child is willing.

Play Tip: Add an element of playfulness by allowing your child to dress in fairy wings.

Loving-Kindness Meditation

The loving-kindness meditation is one known all around the world, and, regardless of the variation, is used as a way of sending loving thoughts to yourself and others. When we send ourselves and others compassion, we tend to feel happier and more grateful. Building an internal sense of self-love and compassion is one of the most crucial aspects of healthy self-image and self-esteem. In the context of this book, it's a great practice to do with your child before bed, or when they've had a hard day.

1. Tell your child that you are going to send kind wishes to someone.

2. Help your child identify someone they want to send kind wishes to.

3. Have your child imagine that person in their mind as they send them the wishes below:

    May you be safe and loved
    May you be happy and healthy
    May you know that all is well

4. Finally, have your child send the kind thoughts to themselves by repeating the saying again as they think of themselves:

    May you be safe and loved
    May you be happy and healthy
    May you know that all is well

Play Tip: You can practice sending these kind wishes to people you care about, people that annoy you—even everyone in the whole wide world!

Calm Place

The goal of this activity is to help your child imagine a calm, safe place. This type of guided relaxation is great to do before bed or to help your child return to a sense of tranquility after being overwhelmed. Using visualization and imagination to envision ourselves in a calmer state is a powerful way to shift our mood.

MATERIALS: Drawing materials (crayons, markers, paints, and/or colored pencils), glitter, stickers

1. Help your child imagine a calm place that they can draw: *Imagine a calm place where nothing bad can ever happen. This place can be real or imaginary and filled with magical helpers and unlimited magic wishes. Anything goes in this place, as long as it makes you feel calm.*

2. Once your child identifies their calm place, allow them to create an image of it on the following page, using creative materials to help them bring their drawing to life.

3. After the drawing is complete, ask your child to try to imagine the picture by pretending to snap a picture of it with the camera in their mind.

4. Have them close their eyes and try to imagine the calm place, even if their eyes are closed.

Play Tip: Have your child identify a calming smell like lavender or peppermint that they can put in their safe place. Encourage them to smell the calm scent and look at the image they created right before bed.

Mind Jar

In this activity, you and your child will create a tool to use for breathing, soothing, calming, and intentional focus. I learned it from a colleague years ago and have used it with my clients in sessions ever since. (Given the creativity involved, it's also something you might find on Instagram and Pinterest!)

MATERIALS: Mason jar, craft glitter (various colors), glitter glue, water

1. With your child, fill the jar halfway with water.

2. Allow your child to add in as much glitter as they please. Allow for creativity and color mixing!

3. Squeeze in a medium amount of glitter glue. This is not an exact science, but too much glitter glue will not create the right effect. Try starting with three squeezes of the bottle.

4. Fill the rest of the jar with water and secure the lid on tightly.

5. Start shaking the jar vigorously, allowing the glitter and glue to mix in the water.

6. Once the Mind Jar is all mixed up, give it another shake, place it on the counter, and watch the colorful elements in the jar settle into a calm, relaxed state. Encourage your child to take deep breaths as the jar settles.

7. Explain to your child what the Mind Jar represents:

> When the jar is all shaken up, it's really mixed up, moving really fast, and pretty chaotic. This is what it is like inside our brains and bodies when we have a big mixed-up feeling. When we give the jar time and space and take deep breaths with the jar, it can find a calm, still feeling, again.

8. Use this jar as a timer for deep breaths, like when your child is upset and needs time, space, and deep breaths to help them calm down.

Play Tip: Use the jar to play a noticing game. Start by shaking the jar, and as the glitter settles, take turns noticing different things about the jar. For example, notice the different colors of glitter or how different sizes of glitter settle at different speeds.

Scary Monster Spray

Many parents who have anxious children tell me that bedtime is a difficult time for their child. This activity is a playful way to engage your child's sense of magical thinking and make them feel more in control of their environment. When we feel more powerful, we are less afraid—and often more likely to fall asleep.

MATERIALS: Spray bottle, stickers, sequins, essential oils (optional)

1. Start by telling your child the story of the monster spray:

    Once upon a time, there was a little boy who was afraid to sleep at night. He was scared because he was convinced that there were monsters in his room waiting to scare him as soon as he fell asleep. The little boy could hardly sleep at all because he was so afraid of the monsters. One day, he learned about the magic of monster spray. He learned that monsters hated monster spray. Just one squirt of monster spray before bed would keep the monsters away all night long! One night before bed, he sprayed the magic monster spray. That night, he felt so strong and brave, he knew that even if a monster came along, he could fight them off with just one squirt of this magic spray.

2. Help your child make their own monster spray by having them decorate the spray bottle with stickers and sequins. (This is because monsters hate pretty things!)

3. Make the monster spray by mixing sequins and essential oils (if using) into water. As you add in the sequins, talk about how they hold magic powers to scare away any monster, no matter the size.

4. Fill the spray bottle with the monster spray.

5. Allow your child to spray it around their room before bed.

Play Tip: You can let your child keep the monster spay in their room, within arm's reach, so if they hear a monster coming, they can fight it off with the spray!

My Magic Breath

The goal of this simple coloring activity is to help your child calm down through the use of extended exhale breaths. The more often we are able to breathe fully and deeply, the more regulated and relaxed we become. Moreover, according to a 2019 paper in the *International Journal of Psychophysiology*, it has been proven that spending two minutes a day performing an extended exhale breath—meaning breathing in for about a count of three and breathing out for about a count of four—actually improves problem-solving skills and work performance.

MATERIALS: Drawing materials (crayons, markers, paints, and/or colored pencils)

1. Explain to your child the magic power of their breath: *If we all learn how to breathe out longer than we breathe in, we can teach our bodies to be calm, strong, and better at making tough choices.*

2. Have them grab their favorite drawing materials and complete the coloring page that follows. Direct them to color along the "inhale" pattern for a count of three while they inhale; direct them to color along the "exhale" pattern for a count of four while they exhale.

3. Repeat the previous step as many times as they like!

Play Tip: Try using this activity before homework, before bed, or when you are otherwise helping your child relax.

INHALE FOR 3 . . . 2 . . . 1 while you color the pattern

EXHALE FOR 4 . . . 3 . . . 2 . . . 1 while you color the pattern

RESOURCES

Websites

Association for Play Therapy: A4PT.org

Little Flower: Children Yoga & Mindfulness Practices: LittleFlowerYoga.com.

National Association for the Education of Young Children: NAEYC.org.

Trust-Based Relational Interaction (TBRI) is a type of parenting framework designed to help meet the specific challenges faced by parents who have children that have experienced trauma. Visit the website to learn more: Child.TCU.edu.

Books

No-Drama Discipline: The Whole-Brain Way to Calm the Chaos and Nurture Your Child's Developing Mind by Daniel Siegel and Tina Payne Bryson

The Out-of-Sync Child: Recognizing and Coping with Sensory Processing Disorder by Carol Stock Kranowitz

The Body Keeps the Score: Brain, Mind, and Body in the Healing of Trauma by Bessel van der Kolk

My Book About Play Therapy by Sandra Wilson

Sitting Still Like a Frog: Mindfulness Exercise for Kids (And Their Parents) by Eline Snel

REFERENCES

Bailey, Becky. *I Love You Rituals*. New York: HarperCollins, 2000.

Bialer, Doreit and Lucy Jane Miller. *No Longer a Secret: Unique Common Sense Strategies for Children with Sensory or Motor Challenges*. Arlington, TX: Sensory World, 2011.

Cochran, Jeff L., Nancy H. Cochran, and William J. Nordling. *Child-Centered Play Therapy: A Practical Guide to Developing Therapeutic Relationships with Children*, Hoboken, NJ: John Wiley & Sons, Inc, 2010.

De Couck, Marijke, Ralf Caers, Liza Musch, Johanna Fliegauf, Antonio Giangreco, and Yori Gidron. "How Breathing Can Help You Make Better Decisions: Two Studies on the Effects of Breathing Patterns on Heart Rate Variability and Decision-Making in Business Cases." *International Journal of Psychophysiology 139* (May 2019): 1–9. DOI.org/10.1016/j.ijpsycho.2019.02.011.

Delahooke, Mona. *Beyond Behaviours: Using Brain Science and Compassion to Understand and Solve Children's Behavioural Challenges*. Eau Claire, WI: PESI Publishing & Media, 2019.

Delahooke, Mona. *Social and Emotional Development in Early Intervention*. Eau Claire, WI: PESI Publishing & Media, 2017.

"The Dream Catcher History & Legend." DreamCatcher.com. Accessed June 14, 2020. dreamcatcher.com/dream-catcher-history-legend.html.

Gaskill, Richard and Perry, Bruce D. "The Neurobiological Power of Play: Using the Neurosequential Model of Therapeutics to Guide Play in the Healing Process." In *Creative Arts and Play Therapy for Attachment Problems*, edited by C. Malchiodi and D. A. Crenshaw, 178–94. New York: Guilford Press, 2013.

Harper, Jennifer Cohen. *Little Flower Yoga for Kids: A Yoga and Mindfulness Program to Help Your Child Improve Attention and Emotional Balance*. Oakland, CA: New Harbinger, 2013.

Leggett, Elsa Soto and Jennifer N. Boswell. *Directive Play Therapy Theories and Techniques.* New York: Springer Publishing, 2017.

"Making Empathy Books." Echo Parenting & Education. YouTube video, 19:54. YouTube.com/watch?v=ruzGK8ySay0&feature=emb_title.

Neuburger, Emily K. *Show Me a Story: 40 Craft Projects and Activities to Spark Children's Storytelling.* North Adams, MA: Storey Publishing, 2012.

Rodwell, Helen and Vivien Norris. *Parenting with Theraplay: Understanding Attachment and How to Nurture a Closer Relationship with Your Child.* Philadelphia: Jessica Kingsley Publishers, 2017.

Striniste, Nancy. *Nature Play at Home: Creating Outdoor Spaces that Connect Children with the Natural World.* Portland, OR: Timber Press, Inc., 2019.

"Tiny Treasures—Loose Parts Play." *Picklebums.* Published July 6, 2016. Picklebums.com/we-play-tiny-treasures.

Turner-Bumberry, Tracy. *2,4,6,8, This is How We Regulate: 75 Play Therapy Activities to Increase Mindfulness in Children.* Eau Claire, WI: PESI Publishing & Media, 2018.

VanFleet, Risë, Andrea E. Sywulak, and Cynthia C. Sniscak. *Child-Centered Play Therapy.* New York: Guilford Press, 2010.

INDEX

ACKNOWLEDGMENTS

I want to take this opportunity to offer my deepest gratitude to my mentors and colleagues in the field of play therapy. I would be nowhere in my career if it wasn't for your guidance, support, supervision, and training. I want to offer a special acknowledgment to my longtime mentor, Ann Beckley-Forest—you have been a special part of my career since before it even began, and I can't thank you enough.

I also want to extend special thanks to my family, without whom I would be lost—especially my husband and daughter. I could say thank you a million times and it still would not be enough. Lastly, I want to acknowledge my first teacher in life, my sweet mother. She was the most playful and loving woman, whose bright light continues to guide my way, even in her absence.

ABOUT THE AUTHOR

Melissa LaVigne is a licensed clinical social worker and registered play therapist. She runs a small private practice in Buffalo, New York, where she provides therapy services to children, families, and adults. She has spent her career honing specialized skills in play therapy and trauma treatment. Melissa is passionate about sharing these tools with the world and, in an effort to do so, trains both nationally and internationally on these topics. In addition to her clinical work, Melissa is a faculty member, trainer, and yoga teacher for Yogis in Service, a nonprofit that brings trauma-informed yoga and mindfulness tools to individuals all over the Buffalo area.